"*Supporting Bereaved Children in the Primary Classroom* is a useful guide for primary school staff seeking to better understand and support bereaved pupils. It brings clarity to a sensitive subject and encourages confident, thoughtful responses to children's grief within the school environment."

**Lorna Vyse**, *Childhood Bereavement Specialist and Children's Author*

"*Supporting Bereaved Children in the Primary Classroom* is a breath of fresh air with its balance of theory and practice, helpful guidance and, above all, a caring approach; essential reading for anyone who works in a primary school."

**Anna Lise Gordon**, *Professor of Education, St Mary's University*

# SUPPORTING BEREAVED CHILDREN IN THE PRIMARY CLASSROOM

Children experience a range of emotions during their time in primary school; however, bereavement is both unique and challenging. This book seeks to enable adults working with children to be prepared for this part of life's journey and ready to support the child affected by the death of their loved one.

This accessible book explores topics that may have not been fully explored during teacher training, including defining loss, grief and bereavement, looking at different models of grief, identifying how grief affects children and investigating how the differing needs of minority groups can be met. Focussed on delivering practical and hands-on guidance, readers are presented with expert advice and case studies from the classroom to understand how to create an effective childhood bereavement policy. Whilst supporting a bereaved child is crucial, the emotional toll on the adult should not be underestimated and this book offers applied self-care strategies tailored for educators. A resource bank with contact details for specialist childhood bereavement organisations is also included for quick reference in a crisis. The authors also make suggestions for play-based activities and guided tasks using high-quality texts for school adults to use in small groups or with the whole class.

This is a much-needed resource for every classroom to best support young people experiencing anxiety, depression and mental health issues after facing a death. This book gives primary teachers, school leaders and staff the confidence to build learning environments that nurture and support students through this difficult time.

**Emma L. Palastanga** is a passionate educator with over 25 years of experience. She has worked in different school settings as a teacher and school leader instigating change. She has also worked as an Ofsted inspector evaluating the quality of education. Emma has lived experience of supporting children after the death of a loved one, and she is keen to empower all staff in primary schools to support children who are bereaved.

**Poppy Gibson** is a lecturer in Education at the Open University, and her research centres around well-being and mental health. After over a decade teaching and leading in primary schools around London, Poppy moved into higher education to work on primary education degrees.

**Marie Greenhalgh** is a former College Headteacher and is now Relationships Director for charity Inclusion Education. She has worked for Inclusion Education for over 16 years building programmes and education provision that support young people with mental health needs and neurodiversity.

# SUPPORTING BEREAVED CHILDREN IN THE PRIMARY CLASSROOM

Helping Children Process Death, Grief and Loss

Emma L. Palastanga, Poppy Gibson and Marie Greenhalgh

Cover image: © Fay Snook

First published 2026
by Routledge
4 Park Square, Milton Park, Abingdon, Oxon OX14 4RN

and by Routledge
605 Third Avenue, New York, NY 10158

*Routledge is an imprint of the Taylor & Francis Group, an informa business*

© 2026 Emma L. Palastanga, Poppy Gibson and Marie Greenhalgh

The right of Emma L. Palastanga, Poppy Gibson and Marie Greenhalgh to be identified as authors of this work has been asserted in accordance with sections 77 and 78 of the Copyright, Designs and Patents Act 1988.

All rights reserved. No part of this book may be reprinted or reproduced or utilised in any form or by any electronic, mechanical, or other means, now known or hereafter invented, including photocopying and recording, or in any information storage or retrieval system, without permission in writing from the publishers.

*Trademark notice*: Product or corporate names may be trademarks or registered trademarks, and are used only for identification and explanation without intent to infringe.

*British Library Cataloguing-in-Publication Data*
A catalogue record for this book is available from the British Library

ISBN: 978-1-032-87332-9 (hbk)
ISBN: 978-1-032-87448-7 (pbk)
ISBN: 978-1-003-53208-8 (ebk)

DOI: 10.4324/9781003532088

Typeset in Interstate
by codeMantra

**This book is dedicated to:**

All those who have felt (and still feel) the pain of bereavement, especially those who are children.

Adults in school who are supporting those grieving, please continue your essential work.

Significant family members we love and mourn.

You have all inspired this book.

# CONTENTS

*Foreword: "Just Say Something!"*   xi
Anna Lise Gordon

*Authors' acknowledgements*   xiii
*Children's voices expressing grief*   xv

1  **Introduction**   1

2  **Loss, grief and bereavement**   7

3  **The way we experience death of a loved one**   15

4  **Stages of grief**   21

5  **How children understand death**   31

6  **Different perspectives on death and the afterlife**   39

7  **Childhood bereavement policy**   46

8  **What can we learn from special schools?**   54

9  **What can we learn from a hospice?**   60

10  **Supporting minority groups**   66

11  **Lived experiences of grief and bereavement**   75

12  **How to support and look after yourself**   81

| 13 | **Resource bank** | 87 |
| 14 | **Conclusion** | 112 |

*Children's advice to school adults* 115
*Index* 117

# FOREWORD: "JUST SAY SOMETHING!"

In my 40-year career in education, as a teacher and teacher educator, the subject of death has rarely been on the professional development agenda for teachers and other adults working in schools. The good news is that this is changing, little by little, and this book is a welcome and much-needed contribution to the growing discussions about how to support bereaved children in our primary schools.

The subject of death, grief and loss is now firmly on the national agenda, with moves towards more overt inclusion in the primary curriculum and in policy and practice discussions, alongside a growing body of rich and thought-provoking research projects with teachers and children. This is part of an unswerving commitment to supporting children affected by a range of adverse childhood experiences, but, even more broadly, it is about equipping ALL children to understand and be confident in talking about loss and bereavement.

Teachers worry about saying the wrong thing, so often say nothing or very little. This is borne out of an understandable desire to protect the child, but my own research (Gordon, 2023) and wider engagement with this topic (Gordon, 2024) has resulted in a resounding message for the profession: "Just Say Something!"

This call to arms echoes throughout this book as the co-authors bring a wealth of knowledge and experience and offer a range of research and evidence-informed perspectives on such an important topic. It is a privilege to be able to learn from the co-authors and other contributors from the primary school classroom and beyond, all specialists in their field, knowledgeable about age-appropriate approaches and strategies that meet the developmental and additional needs of the children.

We do a disservice to children if we continue to brush death, grief and loss under the carpet, as something too 'awkward' to discuss. Work will take time, and this book provides much-needed support for this process of change in how we focus meaningfully on bereavement in primary schools, working with families, hospices and other community organisations. The powerful lived experiences shared in this book shine through as beacons of hope as we strive towards normalising conversations about death, grief and loss in our primary school settings.

This publication is a breath of fresh air with its balance of theory and practice, helpful guidance and, above all, a caring approach. This book gives me a sense of optimism – at an individual and collective level – with its insights into contextual knowledge, stories from the classroom, examples of good practice, policy suggestions and valuable links to a plethora of resources. This book is essential reading for anyone who works in a primary school. As noted in the title of the UK Commission on Bereavement's report (2022), bereavement is everyone's business and we need well-trained professionals in our primary schools, attuned to the individual needs of the children, who have the sensitivity, compassion and courage to just say something!

Professor Anna Lise Gordon<br>March 2025

## Bibliography

Child Bereavement UK. (2018). *Improving bereavement support in schools*. Available at: https://www.childbereavementuk.org/Handlers/Download.ashx?IDMF=fa7a443b-636d-4238-af12-accedec84419.

Gordon, A.L. (2023). *Grief matters: Exploring the impact of bereavement & grief on learning for all*. British Educational Research Association. Available at: https://www.bera.ac.uk/publication/grief-matters.

Gordon, A.L. (2024). *Bereavement in Education Summit Report*. Available at: https://www.stmarys.ac.uk/research/centres/centre-for-wellbeing-in-education/bereavement-in-schools.aspx.

UK Commission on Bereavement. (2022). *Bereavement is everyone's business*. Available at: https://bereavementcommission.org.uk/ukcb-findings/.

# AUTHORS' ACKNOWLEDGEMENTS

I would like to thank first and foremost my wonderful co-authors Poppy and Marie who have shared insights, personal experiences and professional knowledge. It has been a joy to work with you both, sharing our vision and passion to support others with such a sensitive topic. I extend my thanks to all the fantastic contributors who have further enriched this book with their wisdom.

To the publishers who have acknowledged the importance of this subject and the gap we identified, thus enabling this publication to become a reality. Thanks too for suggested improvements along the way.

Thanks to the many people who have supported me in writing this book through gentle encouragement or by sharing their own ideas and allowing me to freely use them in this text. Special thanks to the children (Ben, Emma and James) who have carefully redrawn figures to illustrate key points and those from St Margaret's C of E Aided Junior School in Bideford, Devon (Charlie, Grace, Imogen, Jack, Jacob, Nylah and Willow) who contributed words expressing their feelings after a loved one has died and made suggestions as to what adults in school can do to help children who are bereaved.

Thank you to two specialists in the field of childhood bereavement, Anna Lise Gordon, Professor of Education, St Mary's University, for her wonderful foreword and further reading list, and to Lorna Vyse, Childhood Bereavement Specialist and Children's Author, for her incredibly thorough feedback ensuring that our words were as powerful as our intent and also their valued endorsements of our work.

Last but by no means least I would like to thank my wonderful husband David for his unwavering support and putting up with me locking myself away to write!

**Emma L. Palastanga**

Being part of this book feels so incredibly valuable and I am so grateful to my co-authors Emma and Marie for working with me on this journey and to our amazing contributors who have shared their voices within these pages too.

My father died while I was an ECT, but his values and memories are ones I have always kept with me through my teaching career to date.

Supporting students with death, grief and loss is complex and needs to be handled with sensitivity, care and compassion. Even if this book helps facilitate just one more kind conversation, it has all been worth it!

**Poppy Gibson**

My own journey through grief has profoundly shaped the way I see the world and my role as an educator. Losing my mother at a young age instilled in me a deep understanding of the emotional turmoil that children can experience. This personal experience has driven my passion to advocate for a more compassionate and supportive environment for children dealing with loss. I am immensely grateful for the opportunities I have had to make a difference in the lives of grieving children. Through this book, we aim to provide insights and practical advice for educators, parents and caregivers. My hope is that these tools will help ensure that children feel understood, supported and less alone in their journey. I dedicate this book to all the children who carry loss with them into the classroom. May we continue to build spaces where they are met with compassion, understanding and hope. Let us strive to create environments where their emotional needs are acknowledged and addressed, allowing them to heal and grow.

With deep gratitude,

**Marie Greenhalgh**

# CHILDREN'S VOICES EXPRESSING GRIEF

'Which words best describe how you felt when the person you love died?'

Sad    devastated    heart broken

Jack, aged 9

My baby cousin died.
My Auntie died.
My grandad died.

Jacob, aged 8

I feel sad, gulm, devesated.

Jacob, aged 8

A teacher can help a child when a family member has died by cheering them up.

Nylah, aged 7

My grandad had died so i felt awfully sad.

Imogen, aged 9

My great nan and grandad died when I was 3, I was really sad.

Willow, aged 8

When my great uncle died i felt heartbreak

Grace, aged 9

# 1 Introduction

## Introduction

*One child in every UK classroom will experience bereavement by the time they reach sixteen years old.*

Grief Encounter (no date)

- Does this fact surprise you?

*The UK Commission on bereavement recommends that children are 'sensitively supported by their school, college or workplace during their bereavement'.*

(UKCB 2022)

- Do you feel well prepared to support the young people in your classroom?

The aim of this book is to support staff in primary schools to feel empowered to support children who are grieving, especially those who are bereaved. You may ask: What is the difference between grief and bereavement? This is something we will explore in more detail in Chapter 2, but in a nutshell, grief is the response we have to any type of loss, bereavement is grief that involves the death of a loved one. If you don't feel prepared to support children dealing with this complex emotion, you are not alone. A report on bereavement among children and young people found that 80% of teachers receive no training on coping with death, bereavement and grief (O'Neill et al., 2018) and teachers report low confidence in this area (McManus and Paul, 2019). Thankfully times are changing; I know that from 2020 all primary and secondary trainee teachers (500+ per year) at St Mary's University, London, receive bereavement awareness training as part of their initial teacher education provision. I strongly believe that bereavement training should be a mandatory element of initial teacher education for *all* providers. This will ensure (over time) that those working in schools have the knowledge and confidence to support children and young people through bereavement and grief. The UK Commission on Bereavement (2022) states, 'Given the numbers of children who will experience bereavement during childhood, there is a strong case for them to learn about some of the common feelings associated with loss'. They also argue that 'a whole school approach is needed: proactive and flexible pastoral support, a system for managing and communicating important information about bereavements, staff training and support, and policy development'.

DOI: 10.4324/9781003532088-1

In a straw poll I conducted, 49% stated that their school does not have a bereavement policy and 12% were unsure if their school did or did not have a policy in place; it raises the question as to whether schools themselves are equipped. I hope this book will serve as a long-term resource so that staff feel prepared in advance of childhood bereavement and bereaved children feel well supported in the immediate aftermath of the death and throughout their time in primary school. I also hope it will serve as a tool in the midst of a crisis to signpost useful texts and organisations.

My motivation for this book is multifaceted. As a young and inexperienced class teacher I did not feel well prepared to support the first child I encountered when I learned that their parent had incurable cancer. A kind governor pointed me in the direction of some helpful books on the topic of death written in a child friendly style, and *Badger's Parting Gifts* by Susan Varley (1987) is still one of the texts I recommend to others in this situation. They also put me in touch with childhood bereavement charities such as 'Winston's Wish' and a local charity 'See Saw'. As a busy teacher there was a lot to navigate with little time to prepare. In subsequent scenarios I felt better prepared, though the challenge when a second child announced the death of his father only a few weeks after the first, was to support the class in their anxieties about their own parents' carers' and guardians' mortality. The children were also confused, as the first father and child were very open, but the second family were much more private about their situation. I had to explain that everyone is different and deals with death in different ways. Different family dynamics adds a level of complexity to supporting children with a 'one size fits all' approach, it doesn't work! Communication between home and school is key and respect is imperative. It is often helpful if the class is made aware so that they can support the child, **but** this must only be shared if it is the family's and child's wishes, it would be wholly inappropriate to share such sensitive information without their consent. It also presents challenges with how you support the rest of the class as they are faced with mortality, some of them perhaps for the first time. In my later years of teaching, a seven-year-old child's mother died from cancer, the family communicated well with the school and I felt able to support the child throughout the grim journey of declining health and subsequent death. He was very vocal and would like to share details of the upcoming funeral with the class, we would make time to discuss it and the class asked very thoughtful questions, however I occasionally helped him to use the correct terminology 'cremated' rather than 'burned', for example, and had to explain the concept of a 'wake' since the children all wanted to attend the 'party' for his mother! It was quite a learning journey and I have lasting memories of releasing a balloon in the playground; as one child started waving, soon the whole class, without uttering a word, all waved to the symbolic balloon. I should be clear that we are not advocating this particular approach due to the negative ecological impact we are now more aware of, but a symbolic, collective 'goodbye' or memorial is a powerful act and one which also enables children to support a bereaved friend.

The impetus for the book was re-ignited recently. A dear friend of mine had two daughters, the eldest of whom had a life-limiting condition. As a concerned mother she had numerous conversations with the younger child's school about training staff and putting support in place in advance of her likely bereavement at a young age. Tragically and suddenly, her ten-year-old daughter died as a result of contracting COVID, leaving the seven-year-old grieving with sadly little input from the school despite the conversations. Time, finances, available staff and appropriate training courses are all challenges for schools and these were some of the reasons cited for the limited support the school was able to give.

This book will support your school to be a 'compassionate community which has the culture, practice and policies in place to support pupils to prepare and cope with bereavement' (Irvine and McEwan, 2024). It is a book to be read in preparation for a life event that will sadly affect each one of us and the children in our schools. After reading, it will leave no adult feeling uncertain about how they might offer comfort and a listening ear giving them the confidence to 'Just say something'. Paige McCarthy, a participant at the Bereavement in Education Summit 2024, who had been bereaved as a child, with hindsight, astutely concluded that 'it wasn't that teachers didn't care, they just didn't know how to start the conversation…we all just need to say something'.

It will also be a book to reach for in times of crisis to answer some of the 'what now?' questions.

As a primary teacher with the lived experiences outlined, not only I knew this book needed to be written but I also knew I couldn't do it alone. This is such an important and sensitive topic; as such it required a strong author team, I was lucky enough to connect to two wonderful individuals: Dr Poppy Gibson and Marie Greenhalgh co-authors of *All the Things They Never Told You about Teaching: Facilitating Conversations Around Sensitive Topics with Our Learners*' (2024). From the subtitle alone I knew these were people who understood mental health issues and the pressure on teachers increasingly having to deal with sensitive issues which they may feel ill-equipped to do. Chapters in their book such as Mental health in our schools, Death and grief and Suicide prevention marked them out as the perfect co-authors for *Supporting Bereavement in the Primary Classroom*.

In addition to this publication both of my co-authors have additional experiences which are invaluable to a book about grief, bereavement and mental health. Poppy is a member of 'The Hope Collective', the goal of which is to 'change the narrative' for young people and focus on solutions, not symptoms, and focus on their hopes for the future. Poppy is also a trained Samaritan and is a lecturer in education with the Open University, holding a doctorate in child psychology and education and a range of several mental health qualifications including an MSc in Mental Health Science and the First Aid in Youth Mental Health Qualification.

Motivated by her own personal experience of her parent dying whilst she was in primary school, Marie Greenhalgh is a Volunteer Community Ambassador for Winston's Wish, a charity that supports grieving and bereaved children, young adults and families. Her mantra of 'Be who you needed when you were younger' runs through her veins. She was previously the Head of Inclusion College, a Specialist Post 16 College, supporting young people with mental health needs. Their aim is to support our students to develop sustainable strategies to manage their mental health and well-being in the future for a happy, fulfilling and independent adult life. Marie has worked for Inclusion Hampshire for over 16 years, an organisation that puts mental health and well-being at the heart of education and support.

The one commonality between all people in all classrooms, in all parts of the world, in any type of setting, is that we will one day all die. By avoiding discussing death and dying, we limit space for supporting grief and loss and reduce understanding of how to develop coping strategies when someone dies. National Association of Funeral Directors President and Funeral Industry Advisor for Child Bereavement UK, John Adams, launched a Parliamentary petition for all school age children to be taught about death, dying and bereavement in schools. He highlights the importance of speaking to children about death and dying before they experience it and is motivated by his own experience of childhood bereavement after his mother died when he was 12. He recognises that adults want to protect children from emotional pain but acknowledges sadness and death of our loved ones is unavoidable; 'it's part of living' he says. 'With the right information and education, young people and children can be empowered', he adds. Although schools provide a key support mechanism for bereaved children, John says that pupils are unlikely to have spent any time learning about death and grief in the 'safe space' of the classroom, and many schools do not have procedures in place when a student suffers a loss. He questions the logic of including 'how life begins' within the Relationship Sex and Health Education (RSHE) curriculum yet conversely not 'equipping young people with the skills and information to comprehend life ending, better preparing them for the emotions that accompany a death'. His petition achieved over 11,000 signatures, which was debated in parliament in December 2024. As a result, a cross-government bereavement group will continue to explore how best to support bereaved children in schools including reviewing the content of the RSHE curriculum regarding death, dying and bereavement and access to childhood bereavement support.

As authors of this book, we agree with much of what John says, in particular, that when children experience the death of someone close: a member of staff, a sibling or parent, schools need to be prepared to respond appropriately to support the young person. Some schools fall short in this regard, while others excel. This book contains valuable chapters that help provide the reader with key definitions, advice, strategies and research, and practical resources that can be quickly utilised in the classroom.

There is a significant need for a book specifically tailored to supporting bereavement in primary school settings for several reasons:

**Lack of resources**: Teachers often lack the necessary resources and training to effectively support students who are dealing with bereavement. While there are resources available for supporting grieving individuals in general, there is a scarcity of materials specifically designed for primary school teachers.

**Unique needs of Primary School children**: Children in primary school have unique developmental needs and understanding of death and loss. They may struggle to comprehend the concept of death, express their emotions or understand how to cope with grief. A book targeted at primary school teachers will address these specific needs and provide practical strategies for supporting grieving pupils in age-appropriate ways.

**Impact on academic performance and well-being**: Bereavement can significantly impact a child's academic performance, behaviour and overall well-being. Teachers play a crucial role in providing support and creating a safe and understanding environment for grieving children but may feel out of their depth to do so. A book tailored to their needs will equip teachers with the knowledge and tools to effectively address these challenges.

**Guidance for classroom management**: Managing a classroom where one or more pupils are grieving requires a unique set of strategies. Teachers need guidance on how to address sensitive topics related to death, create a supportive classroom environment and accommodate the needs of grieving pupils while maintaining a sense of normalcy for the entire class, who may also be struggling with their own sense of grief and understanding of life and death.

**Collaboration with parents, carers and guardians**: Teachers often work closely with parents, carers and guardians to support grieving pupils. This book on supporting bereavement in primary school will provide guidance on how to effectively communicate with families, how children can initiate difficult conversations at home, involve families in the support process and offer resources for continued support outside of the classroom as they also grieve, the ripple effect.

This book's chapters help provide the reader with key definitions, advice, strategies and research, and practical resources that can be quickly utilised in the classroom. Having introduced the co-authors and set out the aims of the book in this first chapter, Chapter 2 encourages the reader to reflect upon the different types of loss that children may experience. There are many types of loss such as moving home, the death of a pet, grandparent, parent, sibling, member of staff or friend. How can we help children to deal with these? Are they different or similar in the emotions they provoke? Chapter 3 hones in on the definition of bereavement and explores bereavement through suicide, after a long illness and sudden death. Grief can take many forms and we will explore these in turn in this chapter: traumatic grief, complicated grief, delayed grief and secondary losses. Stages of grief are explored in Chapter 4 through the lens of a child in primary school and how teachers might see these stages expressed through behaviour and emotions. Chapter 5 delves deeper into how children understand death at different ages and for those with special educational needs and disabilities including those who are neurodivergent. In this chapter we begin to address how adults can support age- and stage-relevant understanding. Children at various stages of development have different understandings of death. Moreover, children do not move abruptly from one stage to the next and the characteristics from each stage may overlap. For example, as preschool-age children (2-5 years) do not easily grasp abstract concepts, it is important that individual children are spoken to about bereavement in concrete terms. Although primary school-age children (6-11) may begin to develop the understanding that death is something that happens eventually to everyone, it may sometimes be regarded as something 'spooky'. It is therefore important to encourage children at this age to express their feelings and understand that what they are feeling is perfectly natural. In Chapter 6 we take a look at death and the afterlife from different perspectives. In times of loss faith can be a great comfort or indeed a challenge. This chapter provides a very brief overview of how the major world religions or those with a Humanist perspective view death, as well as some of the rituals surrounding it that the children in your class may experience or have experienced. We present a very brief summary of the understanding of death from each perspective as well as what happens to the deceased after death in practical terms and the spiritual belief of an 'afterlife'. Chapter 7 provides examples of a 'Bereavement Policy' including how to support children in the immediate aftermath of the loss and in the long term, considering anniversaries, Birthdays and special events such as Christmas, Eid and Hanukkah without the loved one. We look at the benefits of a policy and what should be included, we discuss a suicide postvention plan and why this might form part of the policy. As well as looking inwards to our own practice it is imperative that we learn from others and look outwards. As part of this practice in Chapters 8 and 9 we learn from special schools who educate children with life-limiting illnesses and also from hospice care about how we might support the family around the grieving child.

Since the pandemic, there has been a growing concern about the disproportionate impact of COVID-19 on people from ethnic minority communities. In a recent interim review, Mayland et al. (2021) noted that there is a stark lack of evidence about understanding the role of family, friends and existing support systems in providing bereavement support for these groups. The initial findings concluded that organisations involved with these communities, including schools, need to be more involved when bereavement services are being developed to ensure that pupils get the support they need. In Chapter 10 we look closely at supporting ethnic minority pupils including Roma and Traveller groups as well as prison-experienced families.

It could be argued that the last few chapters are the most important: in Chapter 11 we capture the voices of a bereaved child, parents, carers and guardians, and teachers, asking what worked well and how they would like to see things improved. Chapter 12 focusses on the additional challenges teachers face when supporting bereaved children. It underscores the demanding nature of teaching which already leaves many educators feeling overwhelmed and highlights the importance of teacher well-being. It emphasises that while supporting a bereaved child is crucial, it requires recognising and managing the emotional toll on the teacher and offers practical self-care strategies tailored for educators. Chapter 13 is a resource bank including activities to use in the classroom linked to well-written children's books to support tricky conversations around grief and death as well as signposting the busy teacher to external organisations. Chapter 14 concludes this book and invites you, the reader, to reflect on what you have learnt throughout this text and how you will apply this learning to your own setting.

Self-reflection questions to encourage deeper thinking:

- **What do you understand by the terms 'grief' and 'bereavement'?**
- **Which chapter will you dive into first or will you read cover to cover?**
- **What do you feel are your school's strengths and areas for development?**

## Bibliography

Adams, J. (2022). Opinion: Bereavement education in schools. Available at: https://www.childbereavementuk.org/blog/opinion-bereavement-education-schools (Accessed: 11 June 2025).

Gibson, P. and Greenhalgh, M. (2024). *All the things they never told you about teaching: facilitating conversations around sensitive topics with our learners'*. Routledge

Grief Encounter | Leeds bereavement forum. (no date)). *Grief encounter.* Available at: https://www.griefencounter.org.uk (Accessed: 11 June 2024).

Irvine, C. and McEwan, J. (2024). Compassionate School Communities - Embedding a culture and practice of grief education and bereavement support in educational settings. Marie Curie Northern Ireland Report.Availableat:https://www.mariecurie.org.uk/globalassets/media/documents/policy/n411-compassionate-schools-report-screen-v5.2.pdf (Accessed: 5 January 2025).

Mayland, C.R., Powell, R.A., Clarke, G.C., Ebenso, B. and Allsop, M.J. (2021). Bereavement care for ethnic minority communities: A systematic review of access to, models of, outcomes from, and satisfaction with, service provision. *PLoS One, 16*(6), e0252188.

McManus, E. and Paul, S. (2019). Addressing the bereavement needs of children in school: An evaluation of bereavement training for school communities. *Improving Schools, 22*(1), 72-85. https://doi.org/10.1177/1365480219825540.

O'Neill, J., Rowland, A. and Koehler, K. (2018). *Improving bereavement support in schools*. Available at: https://www.childbereavementuk.org/Handlers/Download.ashx?IDMF=fa7a443b-636d-4238-af12-accedec84419 (Accessed: 2 January 2025).

The UK Commission on Bereavement. (2022). *Bereavement is everyone's business.* Available at: https://bereavementcommission.org.uk/ukcb-findings/; Also https://bereavementcommission.org.uk/ukcb-findings/8-principles-for-change/ (Accessed: 5 January 2025).

Varley, S. (1987). *Badger's Parting Gifts*. Andersen Press.

Winston's Wish. (no date). Available at: https://www.winstonswish.org/ (Accessed: 2 January 2025).

# 2 Loss, grief and bereavement

- Can you define the difference between loss, grief and bereavement?

## Introduction

In this chapter we will explore the definitions of loss, grief and bereavement, where there are similarities there are also distinct differences. The main similarities with loss and bereavement are that they are both emotionally challenging and grief describes our response to loss or bereavement. We often hear phrases such as 'She is grieving', 'The family are grief-stricken', 'he is struggling with grief' or 'they are working through their grief'.

## Loss

It is a sad fact that everyone will experience loss at some point in their life. 'Loss' can mean many things to young children, but all will evoke a pain response.

Loss can be relatively trivial (from an adult perspective) and transient, such as a lost pencil case or special toy which is later found. Many of us will have experienced the raw emotion expressed by the child when 'Ted' or 'Bunny' can't be found and the relief from parents, carers, guardians and child alike when they are reunited. Some loss, even with an inanimate object, is permanent, such as a helium balloon floating up into the sky, never to be seen again or when lost 'Ted' has no happy reunion. These losses are significant in a child's life and are crucial emotional milestones in learning to cope with life events in the future.

Loss can involve friendships. With children finding their feet with relationships there are many fluctuations between best friends, friends and those no longer friends. Anyone with young children or anyone who has worked with them will be familiar with children 'falling out' and the upset this can cause. In addition, moving to a new area can mean losing contact with old friends and familiar faces or friends moving out of the area even if you stay put. This can also apply to the loss of a parent if a couple separates and one parent moves away or if a primary caregiver is unwell in hospital for example. These types of loss may be temporary but considerable.

Loss can of course be more poignant and permanent; I am talking about death. Death of a pet, a famous figure, a member of the local or school community, a distant family member or a loved one closer to home. It is important to use the term 'death' with children too, rather than what is deemed to be a gentler word 'loss'. It is because of the types of losses I

DOI: 10.4324/9781003532088-2

8  *Supporting bereaved children in the primary classroom*

mentioned above that to use the term 'lost' when you mean 'death' is confusing to a child. Will the deceased return if they are merely 'lost'?

## Grief

Grief describes the response to any type of loss and change of circumstance and it can include a range of emotions. It should be noted that grief can occur prior to any loss; in this case we call it 'anticipatory grief' where the individual feels emotions such as sadness and anxiety, since they are aware of an imminent loss. This could be the loss of a friend moving away or a loved one with a life-limiting illness. In fact, in the case of a life-limiting illness, some of the grief is about the changes and losses experienced in the present moment, for example, what the loved one is no longer capable of doing due to declining physical or mental health or the way their appearance has changed or the way they behave differently.

You may have heard the phrase 'stages of grief' and I briefly present here the Kübler-Ross Grief model (Kübler-Ross, 1969): Denial, Anger, Bargaining, Depression and Acceptance. This will be explored in more detail alongside other models in Chapter 3; however, whichever model we look at, it is important to note that there isn't one linear route through grief or stages to be followed in a chronological order, and in fact many people have stated that 'grief is messy' because it is. Kübler-Ross is clear that people can experience different aspects of grief at different times, some people may not experience all aspects of grief and grief may feel different with different losses; however, it is helpful to be aware of the elements of grief which people may experience so I outline them in Figure 2.1 and they will be discussed more fully later in this book.

There is no one way to grieve, it is as personal as the individual who is grieving which in some ways makes it hard, because there isn't a route map to follow or a timescale to reassure us.

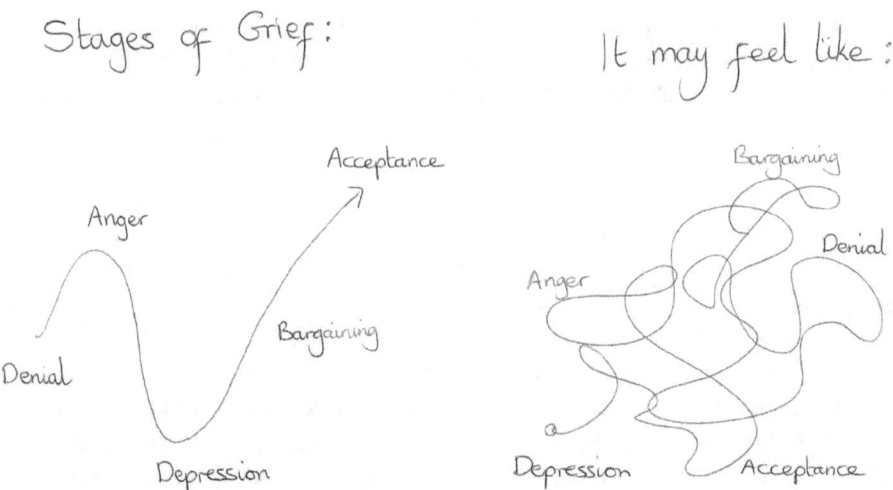

*Figure 2.1* Kübler-Ross Grief model next to a visual representation of how it might feel 'messy'

## Bereavement

There is a difference between grief and bereavement. Bereavement is grief that involves the death of a loved one and it is this that our book will mostly focus on, enabling school staff and other adults to support children through this painful life event.

According to 'Grief Encounter' one child in every UK classroom will experience bereavement by the time they reach the end of secondary school. Grief is 'messy' as we have already discussed; when this grief is in response to the death of a loved one it can be even more complex. There will be many aspects which impact the bereavement including the child's general attitude to life; their mental well-being; their wider supportive relationships; the relationship between the child and the loved one who has died; the circumstances surrounding the death; was it after a long illness, a sudden death through natural causes or even suicide? In a nutshell the journey is unpredictable, and as I stated earlier when discussing grief, every bereavement will be unique to the individuals involved.

For many children, we often assume this loss is likely to be a grandparent or an elderly relative who 'made old bones' and may not come as a huge surprise to the family, but this may well be a significant loss to the child depending on the bond between them, especially if they lived in the same home or were even a primary caregiver. It is crucial to remember that some of the deaths we are considering in a family will be a parent, a sibling who died through miscarriage or stillbirth or even an older sibling such as a child I know who's ten-year-old sister with complex needs died as a result of COVID or a child whose loved one died as a result of suicide. This book will not cover every eventuality, but we hope it will open our readers' minds to the fact that death is a part of life, and any child can be faced with the death of a loved one at any time under any circumstances. We hope our book will give you the knowledge, tools and confidence to support them in navigating this painful experience. This book may trigger your own thoughts and feelings, and this is natural so please take time to look after yourself and skip to Chapter 12 for ideas on supporting yourself as you walk alongside others in their grief and as you read this book.

The idea of supporting a bereaved child may feel daunting, many people worry they may say 'the wrong thing' but saying nothing is far worse. Grief can feel very lonely, confusing and complex, especially to a child. Parminder Sahota, Director of Clinical Services for Grief Encounter (no date), says that 'by listening, validating feelings and being present adults can make an impact on children affected by grief'.

Jill Halfpenny, in her interview with Clare McDonnell for BBC Radio 4's Women's hour about supporting others in grief (21/06/24), states, 'If you can give them your time and you can listen without trying to fix them, that is gold dust'. It is by showing compassion for emotional expression, whether that is tears, anger or seemingly unrelated behavioural changes, making space for grief alongside daily routines and joyous moments and supporting an age-appropriate understanding of death that we can help bereaved children. It is by doing all of this we sprinkle 'gold dust' in dark times.

Whilst supporting a bereaved child, communication and working alongside the child's primary caregiver is of utmost importance, expressing any concerns from school to home and home to school or asking the parent and child what the child would find helpful if they are able to articulate it. Not all requests will be possible to accommodate, but small adaptations such as being able to call home at lunchtime if they are distressed or having a quiet space to gather their thoughts might be a useful starting point. Remember, too, that some families will take great comfort in their faith at a time of loss, whilst others may have no faith or be questioning it, statements such as 'they are in a better place' therefore may not always be helpful. Chapter 6 offers more on this topic.

We often think of grief in the early days of loss and death; however, it should not be underestimated that grief isn't something which fades over time but is something we learn to live alongside and build our lives around, often referred to as 'growing around our grief' and modelled by therapist Lois Tonkin in 1996 with a client when exploring the reality of life after the death of her child. The client drew a circle to represent her life and shaded in how much of this was consumed by grief; 100%. She then drew another circle to represent her imagined future with the size of grief shrinking. When the pair revisited the original diagram after a period of time and re-drew it to represent the reality of life in the present, it looked more like a fried egg: the 'yolk' representing grief and the 'white' with its uneven edges (surrounding the grief) representing life. This concept has since been represented in different ways, my favourite being multiple jars to represent life over time and a ball in each to represent grief. This has been shared on many social media platforms. Instead of the ball of grief diminishing, the jars (life) grow larger to accommodate it (see Figure 2.2).

Twitter user Lauren Herschel introduced me to the idea of 'The ball and the box' (see Figure 2.3). She says that in the beginning the ball is so huge and the box so small that the

*Figure 2.2* Tonkin's model drawn by Emma Brayley aged 11

Figure 2.3 Herschel's 'The ball and the box' drawn by Ben Watson aged 12

ball can't help but bump into the 'pain button' frequently with little control, and to quote her Tweet from December 2017:

> Over time, the ball gets smaller. It hits the button less and less but when it does, it hurts just as much. It's better because you can function day to day more easily. But the downside is that the ball randomly hits that button when you least expect it.

I like to combine these two analogies and say that grief stays the same, it does not diminish but our life/the jar/the box expands, giving us more room for the rest of life, the grief is still painful, but it hits the pain button less frequently and over time we learn strategies to cope. I, for one, tend to have a 'big cry' the tears just flow whenever the intense emotions come up, it is not really by active choice, it just happens but then I feel better for it, I dust myself off, pick myself up and keep going until the next unannounced emotional wave overwhelms me. I'm not saying I don't have tearful episodes in between but these are usually only for a few moments and when met with kindness and understanding from others around me they are short-lived expressions of my ongoing sadness regarding the death of my Dad. Personally, I feel forever changed since his death. I am not physically much different, but I feel different inside and so much around me does too, I am like a jigsaw with a piece missing, but I take comfort from his character and strength and try to use this in my daily life, wearing the comment, 'You're just like your Dad' like a badge of honour!

With this in mind, Anniversaries of the death; religious festivals such as Eid or Christmas, Mothers' Day, Fathers' Day and of course Birthdays, both of the child and the deceased can be very painful reminders of the loss, a time when that ball hits the pain button hard. Sometimes just a smell, a song or a memory can trigger emotions and understanding this in long-term grief as well as normalising this can be a great relief to those struggling with it.

This is the perfect point to note the guilt or distress that is often felt during moments of joy, as though we are forgetting the loved one or that their loss no longer matters because we experience moments of happiness. As the class teacher I remember seeing children enjoying themselves, laughing and generally having a good time when one child started crying for no clear reason at first. When I spoke to them, they explained that they felt 'bad' for laughing because they should be sad after their Mum died. Many adults feel this way too so it must be even more confusing for a child. I explained to the child that emotions connected with grief are like puddles and we jump in and out of the sad feelings and that it is ok to have happy times in between the puddles. 'Puddle Jumping' is explained in a fantastic animation on the Child Bereavement UK website.

I have so far focussed on grief in the single bereaved person, but it should be noted this can have a ripple effect on the rest of the class as they experience mortality, perhaps for the first time, which can trigger feelings of anxiety about their own loved ones. This must be managed sensitively and for young children using a story such as *Badger's Parting Gifts* by Susan Varley or *The Invisible String* by Patrice Karst can be great starting points. Take a look in the resources chapter for activities matched to these books and more. I would also recommend making parents, carers and guardians aware that you will be discussing death in class so that if any questions should come up at home, parents, carers and guardians are forewarned, in the same way you might for sex education. If it is a death within the school community, this will be a shared grief on a much larger scale but just as upsetting for those involved. In this case, perhaps a shared act of condolence such as a memorial garden, a notable tree or a quiet space for reflection for those who knew the deceased? This will be discussed further in Chapter 5 as we explore how children understand death.

Sometimes grief can be defined as 'complicated grief' where a 'bereaved person appears to be 'stuck' in their grief…like grief has become their way of life' (cruse.org.uk). Ernstmeyer and Christman (2021) expanded further on different types of grief:

- **Chronic Grief**: Normal grief reactions that do not subside and continue over very long periods of time.
- **Delayed Grief**: Normal grief reactions that are suppressed or postponed by the survivor consciously or unconsciously to avoid the pain of the loss.
- **Exaggerated Grief**: An intense reaction to grief that may include nightmares, delinquent behaviours, phobias and thoughts of suicide.
- **Masked Grief**: Grief that occurs when the survivor is not aware of behaviours that interfere with normal functioning as a result of the loss.

Cruse.org.uk states that different factors can increase the risk of complicated grief: factors such as the relationship to the deceased (for example, the death of a parent or sibling) and the circumstances of the death (if it was sudden or unexpected or perhaps a result of suicide which may also be impacted by social stigma). If a child has experienced multiple losses (not necessarily through death), if they struggle with mental health problems and also their living conditions (perhaps poverty, cultural isolation or exposure to substance misuse) and strength of their support network.

Complicated grief can be difficult to identify but behaviours such as difficulty accepting the death, struggling to trust others, wanting to be alone much of the time (even away from loved ones), feeling uneasy or even negative about the future and feeling agitated are some signs to look out for. Continue to support the bereaved child by encouraging them to talk about their feelings if you can, but complicated grief may require professional assistance depending on its severity. Do not be afraid to encourage the parents, carers and guardians to speak to their GP regarding their child's struggles and I would urge you to turn to Chapter 13 where we signpost further resources such as organisations who can offer specialist support.

## Conclusion

Bereavement will affect approximately 1 in 30 children before they are 16, each person's loss will be felt differently depending on a number of factors, but the compassion and empathy (the gold dust) shown by others, both adults and classmates, will help children in this vulnerable state to navigate one of life's most complex experiences.

Self-reflection questions to encourage deeper thinking:

- **How would you define loss, grief and bereavement?**
- **Are there similarities between them?**
- **What are the key differences?**

## Bibliography

Ernstmeyer, K. and Christman, E. (Eds.). (2021). Chapter 17 Grief and Loss. In *Nursing Fundamentals*. Available at: https://www.ncbi.nlm.nih.gov/books/NBK591827/ (Accessed: 12 August 2024).

Kübler-Ross, E. (1969). *On Death and Dying* (1st ed.). Routledge. https://doi.org/10.4324/9780203010495.

Tonkin, L. (1996). Growing around grief—Another way of looking at grief and recovery. *Bereavement Care*, *15*(1), 10. https://doi.org/10.1080/02682629608657376 (Accessed: 9 August 2024).

## Websites

Child Bereavement UK. (2022). *Puddle Jumping* [online]. Available at: https://www.childbereavementuk.org/puddle-jumping (Accessed: 4 August 2024).

Cruse Bereavement Support. (2021). *Complicated grief in children* (no date). Available at: https://www.cruse.org.uk/understanding-grief/grief-experiences/children-young-people/complicated-grief-children/ (Accessed: 6 July 2025).

*Grief Encounter | leeds bereavement forum*. (no date). *Grief encounter*. Available at: https://www.griefencounter.org.uk (Accessed: 10 July 2024).

*Winston's Wish*. (no date). Available at: https://www.winstonswish.org/ (Accessed: 4 August 2024).

# 3 The way we experience death of a loved one

- How does it feel to lose and grieve?
- What sort of behaviours might be expressions of grief?

## Introduction

Each year approximately 50,000 children experience the death of a parent in the UK (Childhood Bereavement Network, 2022), with an even greater number experiencing bereavement in other contexts, such as the death of a grandparent or sibling, peer or pet loss. Previous research on childhood bereavement indicates that such experiences can negatively impact educational attainment, the child's well-being and mental health (either/or near the time of death and later in life) and social relationships (Draper and Hancock, 2011); they may also be more likely to be in contact with the criminal justice system (CYCJ, 2019). Childhood bereavement can therefore directly and indirectly (considering social determinants) impact one's health.

> In previous research, it has been established that a child who has experienced the death of a parent is vulnerable to a variety of concerns, including grief, distress and dysphoria, particularly in the first year following the death.
> 
> (Draper and Hancock, 2011)

## The interchangeability of bereavement and grief

Building on the conversations from the previous chapter around bereavement and grief, what is your opinion? Are these terms interchangeable, and if not, what is the difference between them?

There are different types of bereavement, just as there are different types of grief: traumatic grief, complicated grief, delayed grief and secondary losses. Bereavement and grief are often used interchangeably, but they have distinct meanings. Bereavement refers to the state of loss after a loved one has died, the objective fact of the loss. Grief is the emotional response to that loss. It's the subjective experience of sadness, anger, guilt and other feelings that arise from bereavement. While bereavement is a universal experience, grief is highly individual and varies from person to person.

## What bereavements may children experience?

Children can experience bereavement in a variety of ways, including:

- Death of a parent or carer: this is a significant loss that can have a profound impact on a child's emotional and psychological development.
- Death of a sibling: losing a sibling can be equally devastating, as it disrupts the family dynamic and can lead to feelings of isolation and loneliness.
- Death of a grandparent or other close relative: while not as immediate as the loss of a parent or sibling, the death of a grandparent or other close relative can still be a significant loss for a child.
- Death of a pet: for many children, pets are cherished members of the family, and their loss can be deeply felt.
- Sudden or traumatic death of someone in the child's network: when a death is sudden or traumatic, it can be particularly difficult for children to understand and process.
- Prolonged illness: If a loved one suffers from a long-term illness, children may experience anticipatory grief, as they may know that the loss is inevitable.

## Grieving behaviours

As you have already gathered from reading this book so far, grief is a highly personal and often unpredictable process. We must remember that children grieve in their own way, and their reactions may vary depending on their age, personality and relationship with the person or animal that has died. The amount of information that a child has been given about the death and the clarity of the language used can also impact the child. Some children may express their grief openly, while others may withdraw or become more subdued. It is essential to provide children with support and understanding during this difficult time. The clearer the use of language such as using the word 'died' rather than 'lost' can alleviate anxieties as can avoidance of euphemisms such as 'gone to sleep' which are seen by some as more gentle but are more likely to unwittingly provoke anxiety.

Before we dive into the grief theories, found later in Chapter 4, let us consider some of the emotions – and subsequent behaviours – that children and young people may feel and exhibit when grieving.

## Social aggression

The inability of children to comprehend and process death due to factors like chronological age, attachment of the child to the deceased, nature of death and family support might lead to delayed or prolonged grief processes resulting in complicated grief (CG). Complicated grief in a child's life can affect his/her social and cognitive functioning manifesting in antisocial behaviours. This study aimed to find out antisocial behaviours that are more prevalent among children with complicated grief in selected public primary schools in Nairobi County, Kenya. 259 pupils aged 10-13 years whose loved one had died in the last year. Purposive sampling was also used to select 22 class teachers of the bereaved pupils who participated in the study. The most prevalent antisocial behaviour among these children was social aggression. The study recommends that the Ministry of Education should introduce a school-based counselling programme incorporating grief intervention techniques and recommend trained counsellors who do not double up as teachers to be school counsellors to negate dual relationships. Public primary schools are encouraged to develop several training programmes to help teachers understand how to intervene and foster resiliency in their students who have experienced grief (Omucheni et al., 2024).

## Guilt and shame

An understanding of guilt, shame and other common reactions as well as an appreciation of the role of secondary losses and the unique challenges facing children in communities characterised by chronic trauma and cumulative loss will help the paediatrician to address factors that may impair children's adjustment and to identify complicated mourning and situations when professional counselling is indicated (Schonfeld et al., 2024).

## Isolation, loneliness and feeling ignored

Semi-structured interviews ($N=13$) with adults who experienced a significant bereavement in childhood took place, which involved open-ended questions that were guided by a systematic review of the literature and a meaning-making theoretical framework. Following thematic analysis, five overarching themes were evident: (a) bereavement is an isolating and lonely experience, (b) grief changes the family unit, (c) you feel ignored in school, (d) everything changes and (e) milestones and triggers are lifelong. Recommendations for school staff are also made by participants in terms of acknowledging death, giving children choice in the support they are given, and training school staff to be aware of triggers and milestones (e.g. Mother's Day and Father's Day as mentioned earlier in the book) (Lynam and Mc Guckin, 2025).

More research is urgently needed to enhance knowledge about the interaction between grief reactions of children and their caregivers, to inform the development of interventions promoting adaptive grieving in children (Boelen and Spuij, 2024).

Stylianou and Zembylas (2018) conducted an action research study with children aged 10 and 11 years old in a school in Cyprus where they made space to speak about the concepts of 'grief' and 'grieving' to see the influence this may have on the children's understanding and feelings around death. The findings showed this conversation had a constructive impact on children's understanding of grief and grieving along two important dimensions: 'First, the intervention helped children better define emotional responses to loss (grief); second, children seemed to overcome their anxiety while talking about grief and grieving and were able to share relevant personal experiences' (Stylianou and Zembylas, 2018:1). This action research offers a key consideration for practitioners and policy makers as well as the value in providing sessions around grief and death in teacher training programmes.

## Ways to support children who are feeling and experiencing the death of a loved one

We will touch on this throughout this book but at this point, some simple ways that adults can help to support children and young people when they experience the death of a loved one is really through validating their feelings, whatever those feelings may be. Children need to know that it is normal to feel sad, angry or confused. Practitioners are well-placed to reassure them that their feelings are valid and that it's okay to express them. Children may need time to process their grief, and around this, the child's family may also be dealing with their own grief which will have a secondary impact on the child. Remember, every child is different, and we can't say this enough, there is no one-size-fits-all approach to talking about death. The most important thing is to be open, honest and supportive.

In the following contribution, Erin Skelton, Chief Strategy Officer, Bright Field Consulting, offers insight into death and grief from the perspective of a teacher in Religious Studies (RS).

### Unique experiences, by Erin Skelton, Head of Religious Studies at Worksop College, Coach and Educational Consultant

As an RS teacher, I frequently reflect on the concept of life's journey. The beliefs, choices and rituals that shape our values, identity, vulnerability and empathy are central to our shared humanity. My aim is for every child who enters my classroom to engage with and understand these foundational aspects of life.

I am constantly inspired by my students – their resilience, wisdom and the joy they bring, even when facing life's most difficult challenges. In shaping my approach to teaching these profound topics, I often draw upon my own experiences of childhood bereavement to guide best practice.

Bereavement manifests in many forms, and a child's response cannot be reduced to a single narrative or set of emotions. For many, their first encounter with loss may be the death of a grandparent, the passing of a beloved pet, the separation of caregivers or a significant relocation. Some experience multiple losses in quick succession, which can profoundly affect their emotional and physical well-being, sometimes well into adulthood. Conversely, some children may reach late adolescence before facing a significant bereavement, which can shape their experience of grief differently.

For some, the process of grief begins long before death occurs. In larger, close-knit families, younger children may accompany caregivers on visits to hospitals, care homes or palliative facilities. This prolonged exposure can heighten their anxiety – not only about the impending loss of their loved one but also about their own mortality. In some cases, this may result in PTSD or CPTSD. Others may experience a sudden, unexpected bereavement, grappling with the shock and struggling with questions of 'what if' or regret over not having had the chance to say goodbye.

Adult caregivers often lack the tools to support grieving children effectively. Their own complex emotions can leave children as passive observers within the family dynamic. In some cases, children even inherit grief from bereavements that occurred before their birth or adoption. These children frequently express a deep, inexplicable sense of sadness or loss tied to events they never directly experienced.

Cultural and religious backgrounds can have a profound impact on how children process grief. Each child's understanding of loss is influenced by the beliefs and traditions they are raised with, and these can shape their emotional responses and rituals. For example, some cultures have specific mourning periods, practices or ways of remembering loved ones that provide comfort and structure. It's essential for us, as educators, to recognise the diversity of experiences in our classrooms, ensuring that we approach grief with sensitivity to the cultural and religious contexts that may be at play. Chapter 6 provides an overview of religious views on death and outlines some of the rituals a child from a particular faith may have experienced.

Grieving children may hesitate to share their feelings with caregivers, fearing they'll add to the family's burden. Instead, they often turn to other outlets, confiding in friends and toys or seeking solace at school.

Caregivers also differ in their approaches to rituals around death and funerals. Some exclude children from these rituals to shield them from trauma, while others include them in open-casket viewings or cremation ceremonies. What's most important is that children are given the opportunity to grieve in ways appropriate to their emotional and intellectual maturity. They need spaces to say goodbye, to remember and to talk about their loved ones.

Working with specialist childhood bereavement practitioners (those trained in supporting childhood bereavement) or bereavement counselling are areas often overlooked. Many children – and their caregivers – are not offered the chance to work with professionals who can help them process their grief. Regardless of age, children may struggle to articulate the emotions they are experiencing, making professional support an invaluable resource.

Grief doesn't simply disappear after a funeral or memorial. While it's often assumed that children will bounce back after a loss, the truth is that unresolved grief can linger, affecting their emotional development and relationships well into adulthood. Grief can subtly shape how children view themselves and the world around them. If not addressed, it can manifest in ways that influence their mental health, their ability to trust or even how they engage in future relationships. By supporting children through their grief, we not only help them in the immediate aftermath but also lay the groundwork for them to grow into resilient, empathetic adults.

As teachers, we inevitably encounter childhood loss and bereavement as part of our role. In these moments, it is crucial to empathise with our students and not shy away from sharing how grief, loss or bereavement has impacted us personally. By offering students the opportunity to feel seen and heard and helping them connect with others who have faced similar experiences, we provide a valuable space for healing and understanding. Ultimately, the way we guide children through the experience of grief shapes their ability to develop resilience and empathy throughout their lives. This is a responsibility we must approach with great care and compassion.

## Conclusion

Children may experience death and loss in many places with many people. Considering these different connections and severances of connections, how they may look for young people may help practitioners to make space to talk about feelings and work towards processing the grief. The following chapter will look at four models of grief to help offer frameworks that may be useful for consideration of the phases of grief.

Self-reflection questions to encourage deeper thinking:

- **What are some of the deaths and losses that children may suffer?**
- **How can we open up spaces to talk about death?**
- **What role should practitioners play when it comes to supporting children who are grieving?**

## Bibliography

Boelen, P.A. and Spuij, M. (2024). Individual and systemic variables associated with prolonged grief and other emotional distress in bereaved children. *Plos One*, 19(4), e0302725.

Childhood Bereavement Network. (2022). Based on 2019-2021 data and key statistics 2022. Available at: https://www.childbereavementuk.org/death-bereavement-statistics.

CYCJ. (2019). *Bereavement and offending behaviours: A role for Early and Effective Intervention (EEI)?* Available at: https://www.cycj.org.uk/wp-content/uploads/2019/10/Bereavement-and-EEI-1.pdf.

Draper, A. and Hancock, M. (2011). Childhood parental bereavement: The risk of vulnerability to delinquency and factors that compromise resilience. *Mortality*, 16(4), 285-306. https://doi.org/10.1080/13576275.2011.613266.

Lynam, A.M. and Mc Guckin, C. (2025). 'People ignore you because they are afraid...': retrospective school and life experiences of individuals who were bereaved in childhood. *Pastoral Care in Education*, 1-19. https://doi.org/10.1080/02643944.2025.2464532.

Omucheni, P.N., Mwenje, M. and Kamunyu, R. (2024). Antisocial behaviours that are more prevalent among children with complicated grief in selected public primary schools in Nairobi County, Kenya. *Journal of Sociology, Psychology and Religious*, 4(5), 18-32.

Schonfeld, D.J., Demaria, T., Nasir, A. and Kumar, S. (2024). Supporting the grieving child and family: Clinical report. *Pediatrics*, 154(1), e2024067212.

Stylianou, P. and Zembylas, M. (2018). Dealing with the concepts of "grief" and "grieving" in the classroom: Children's perceptions, emotions, and behavior. *OMEGA - Journal of Death and Dying*, 77(3), 240-266.

# 4 Stages of grief

- What are the different stages of grief and how might this be expressed by children in school?

## Introduction

This chapter will begin by presenting four theorists and their grief models that have contributed to the current understanding of the stages of grief: Elisabeth Kübler-Ross, John Bowlby, Colin Murray Parkes and George Bonanno Dennis Klass. As you read through these four models and theories, consider your personal encounters with death and loss and reflect upon which, if any, best fit your lived experiences.

## Elisabeth Kübler-Ross

Perhaps the most well-known theorist and one we briefly introduced you to in Chapter 2 is Kübler-Ross who introduced the 'Five Stages of Grief' model in her 1969 book *On Death and Dying* (Kübler-Ross, 1969). Kübler-Ross said we move through the stages like this:

1. Denial: we may feel shock, confusion and fear at the news someone has died.
2. Anger: we may feel frustrated, irritated and anxious that they have died.
3. Bargaining: at this midpoint of the grief journey, we may feel overwhelmed, helpless or hostile towards others.
4. Depression: we may struggle to find meaning but may begin telling our story or reaching out to others for support.
5. Acceptance: at this final fifth point, we may begin moving on with a new plan in place.

While widely recognised, it's important to note that these stages aren't necessarily experienced in a linear or sequential manner, refer back to Figure 2.1 in Chapter 2, which represents how these stages might be experienced.

## George Bonanno

Dr George Bonanno's research challenges the idea of a single, linear grief process, and he refutes the idea of the five stages of grief (Bonanno, 2009). According to Bonanno, the bereaved exhibit different patterns of grief reactions across time, ranging from overwhelming feelings of loss for long periods of time (more than two years) to less pronounced feelings of sadness over a year or less. Bonanno talks about a 'grief trajectory model' which has four distinct trajectories that bereaved individuals may follow: resilience, chronic grief, delayed grief and recovery. This model emphasises the importance of recognising and respecting individual differences in the grief process.

## John Bowlby and Colin Murray Parkes

These theorists proposed a model on 'the four phases of grief' that emphasises the importance of attachment and loss in the grieving process; this builds on Bowlby's previous work around the importance of attachments in our early lives (Parkes, 1998). Their grief model includes four phases: Shock and Numbness, Yearning and Searching, Disorganisation and Despair, and Reorganisation.

**Shock and Numbness**: This initial phase is characterised by a sense of disbelief and emotional detachment, often described as feeling numb or unable to process the loss.
**Yearning and Searching**: In this phase, individuals experience intense longing for the deceased and may engage in behaviours aimed at finding or recreating the person who has died or the relationship which has significantly changed.
**Disorganisation and Despair**: As the reality of the loss sets in, individuals may experience feelings of sadness, anger, guilt and confusion, potentially leading to withdrawal from daily activities and hobbies.
**Reorganisation and Recovery**: This phase involves adjusting to a new reality without the deceased, gradually finding new meaning and purpose in life and accepting the changes that have occurred.

Bowlby and Parkes' model, emphasising attachment and loss in grief, has been criticised for its linear, stage-based approach, which doesn't account for individual variability and the complexity of grief experiences.

## Dennis Klass

Klass focusses on the concept of 'complicated grief', which involves intense and sustained grief, used synonymously with 'prolonged grief' that interferes with daily functioning (Kastelnik, 2024). He highlights the importance of social support and professional help in coping with complicated grief (Klass et al., 1996).

## Stroebe and Schut

Stroebe and Schut's 'Dual Process Model' (1999) identifies two types of focus or 'zones' labelled 'loss' and 'restoration'. The key learning point is that a grieving individual can, and indeed will, move back and forth between the two zones. This is what is meant by 'puddle jumping' which is referred to in Chapter 2. This model explains that at times the griever confronts the difficult tasks and emotions associated with grieving and at other times they avoid it and focus on other areas of life. It suggests that taking respite from grieving and oscillating between the two zones is a healthy way to adapt to loss, address it and cope with everyday life.

### Real-world experiences

It's important to remember that these models are frameworks to help understand the grieving process, not rigid rules. Grief is a highly individual experience, and people may move through different stages at their own pace and in their own way.

In the following contribution, Professor Erna Haraldsdóttir and Dr. Suzie Dick share further reflections on grief and loss along with two short case studies.

## Author biographies

Professor Erna Haraldsdóttir BSc, MSc, PhD Nursing

Erna has worked in palliative care since the late 1980s. She was instrumental in developing and setting up a palliative care service within the National Health Care system in Iceland between 1990 and 2000. Erna is Professor in nursing, Deputy Head of nursing and Director of the Centre for Person-centred Practice Research at Queen Margaret University. Erna has extensive experience and knowledge in person-centred palliative care. She leads person-centred practice development, education and research in hospice and palliative care in partnership with Queen Margaret University. She serves on a number of development groups in relation to palliative care education and research and has published widely in palliative care research journals. She has also taken part in developing and delivering national and international teaching programmes in palliative care including Iceland, the UK, Serbia, Uganda and India.

Dr Suzie Dick BSc, PGDE, MSc, MSc, EdD

Suzie is a lecturer in education at Queen Margaret University. She is a strong proponent of grounded theory methodology in relation to understanding lived experiences in education and is lead on the Scottish Grounded Theory Network. Her current research focusses on issues around rural education, place-based education and equity of opportunity and is currently the vice chair of the International Professional Development Association (Scotland). In her other professional life, she is a current Remote Emergency Medical Technician with Scottish Mountain Rescue. Suzie is qualified as a Wilderness Emergency Medical Technician with the Faculty of Wilderness Medicine and has lived and worked around the world including Ethiopia, Austria and Mongolia.

## The grieving process

**Prof. Erna Haraldsdottir, Director of Centre for Person Centred Practice Research, Queen Margaret University, & Dr. Suzie Dick, Lecturer in Education, Queen Margaret University**

### Grief as 'normal' reaction to loss

Contemporary society often seems to want to protect the emotional impact of loss with the notion that children need and should be protected from experiencing strong negative emotions that are provoked by loss. However, loss and grief are part of human experience. Loss is generally experienced by grief, felt deeply in emotions, present in our thoughts and can often be seen in behaviour (Arizmendi and O'Connor, 2015).

Theories of grief reaction with grief seen as a 'normal process' for adults started to develop in the mid-1940s. Focus on children in grief followed on from this, demonstrating that children, like adults, have what can be seen as 'normal' grief reactions to loss that serves the same process as in adults, namely to work through the grief towards gaining psychological adjustment and acceptance of the loss. As for adults, the main process involves expression of emotions whereby 'healthy' grieving has been associated with individuals coming to terms with the finality of the loss and integrates this acceptance into their lives (Pomeroy et al., 2011).

### Supporting healthy grieving within the primary school context

How a child copes and adapts to loss through the grieving process is a combination of personal strength and vulnerability and ongoing support from their families, friends and community network. Most bereaved children rely on family and personal resources to deal with loss and do not require professional help (Holland, 2008).

Disclosure of emotional and cognitive experiences of grief constitutes healthy adjustment following a loss. The school community, and it can be argued, should play an important role in providing support for primary school children. It is an environment whereby they can be supported through the process of finding a pathway for their reaction to loss to be expressed. As highlighted in the curriculum of excellence, learning skills and strategies to support children to go through loss and change is one of expected mental and health and well-being outcomes. It is important for primary schools to develop practices that can contribute to recognising and legitimising grief as well as authorising emotional expression and experience around loss and supporting health grieving processes for children within the school community who experience loss. Some primary schools have developed bereavement policies to support their practices.

---

**Case study - lived experience**

*What I wish my school knew*

*I was 7 when my mother died, leaving me orphaned. She had had breast cancer since I was a baby and it was not a surprise to me, I had grown up knowing she would die, and what the plan was for me when it happened. But no-one asked me. I learnt to say the word 'chemotherapy' by saying 'cream of therapy' (I still say that in my head to this day) and seeing the radiotherapy machine and the mask (the mask still haunts me). I remember being told she had died, it was in the summer holidays, at the hospice - I didn't go and visit while she was there, I assume people thought it was too traumatic.*

> *But no-one asked me.*
> *School returned the week after the funeral. There was a school with my friends in it at the bottom of the hill of my new home but it was decided for continuity I would still continue at the old school, a mile way, across a busy main road, a long walk for a seven-year-old by themselves. Would be too many changes they thought. But no-one asked me (I really wanted to go to the school down the hill!). At school, nothing was said until mother's day cards when they said I could do something different. I was made to change my surname, which incidentally has caused me problems to this day in proving my identity. But no-one asked me.*
> *I was never talked to, asked what I wanted, where I wanted to live, what I thought. I didn't know until over 20 years later about the lovely letter my teacher had written to us.*
> *I realised then, that I also owned nothing of my mum's. No-one talked to me about the death, my thoughts, feelings, worries. The takeaway for you as a teacher, school teacher or teaching assistant - every child needs that space to talk, have an opinion, be listened to. If the family can't, remember they are likely never to have been in this situation before, then the school must, don't assume someone else has. No child is 'too young', don't underestimate that need or want to have a say.*

## How children grieve

It is important to consider whilst children can grief and work through the grieving process, the way children experience loss differs from adults and depends on their age and stage in development. Primary age school children can understand the irreversibility of the loss and can understand the permanence of death. Their conception may still be very concrete, and they may have problems with abstract thinking in relation to death and dying. This age group of children can benefit from very factual information and be honest in a concrete way and using observable examples (Cronin Favazza and Munson, 2010).

## Supporting children going through loss and bereavement in primary school

- Support open and honest conversations, communicate clearly and avoid using euphemisms such as 'gone to sleep' or talk about loss. Use straightforward words like die, death and dead. Answer questions as openly and honestly as you can, if you don't know the answer say you will try and find out and liaison with the family of the child as and if needed.
- Don't make assumptions if you are unsure about something the child says, talk it through with them and their family.
- Create an environment whereby loss can be expressed and supported - allow expression of emotions, thoughts and questions, using creative ways of doing this can be helpful and there are a number of resources available to support this.

- Be aware of themes or topics that might cause strong feelings or be upsetting. Prepare for a significant date that may be difficult. In collaboration with the family, plan how the child can be supported on key dates that may be particularly challenging.
- Maintaining the boundaries that existed prior to the loss/death of a loved one around what is acceptable and what is not is important to help this age group to feel safe and secure. Teachers might adjust some expectations for schoolwork, but it is helpful for children to have a certain level of responsibility and routine so that they understand that life will go on despite their loss. Children may also need additional help with school tasks and activities.

> **Case study of good practice using creativity**
>
> *Bereavement boxes in a 3-18 school on a Scottish island*
>
> *This project started through a conversation with the school nurse, following the death of a child's father. While discussing supports, the discussion moved round to all the cards and flowers that went to the family on the island, but nothing specifically for the child themselves. Their needs were often swallowed up in the cultural traditions of how a community behaves following a death. With the help of pupils in the school's well-being centre we began collecting items to go in the bereavement boxes, taking advice from Winston's Wish and a Seasons for Growth facilitator who lived in the community. Into the box went a range of items for keeps sake, including a picture frame, worry doll, memory box and card, and other items, adapted depending on the age and stage of the child. The benefit of being a small community is that we knew when a death had occurred and who it would be appropriate to send the box(es) to. We wanted them to know that as the school was a part of the community that was specifically a large part of their life, we were there for, and remembered them.*

## Resource signposting

Managing Bereavement: A guide for Schools, Child Bereavement UK

Child Bereavement UK https://www.childbereavementuk.org/primary-schools

Developing Bereavement policy https://www.childbereavementuk.org/developing-a-bereavement-policy

Winston Wish https://winstonswish.org/supporting-you/support-for-schools/

Curriculum for Excellence Health and Wellbeing https://education.gov.scot/curriculum-for-excellence/curriculum-areas/health-and-wellbeing/

Fischy Music Resources https://www.fischy.com/fischy-music-online/song-playlists/remembrance-health-wellbeing/

In the second contribution within this chapter, Chris Passey FCCT, Deputy Head of Kimichi School and Co-Founder of EduPulse, shared his own personal experiences with death, and how these helped feed into the understanding and support for children and young people within educational settings.

## Time, space and language: the tools in supporting the stages of grief

### Chris Passey, Deputy Head, Kimichi School

Grieving children prefer the support of their known school teachers over that of prescribed psychological intervention (Frei-Landau, 2023), and we should be embracing this knowledge when faced with the myriad challenges in our daily work.

My first grandparent died when I was 10. It was a confusingly slow yet rapid decline that only the cruelties of breast cancer can bestow on a person. I'm nearly 40 years old and struggle to recall specific details of this very specific childhood trauma and have always wondered if it was my brain playing tricks or otherwise protecting me from the horrors I was witnessing. Di Giuseppe et al. (2021) found that childhood trauma can cause adverse personality development but whether or not my body protected me is another story. In a study of the children of the 2004 Tsunami, 97% of children who recorded indirect memories of the tsunami did so from an onlooker point of view, as opposed to the 63% that observed it directly (Dawson and Bryant, 2016). What does this say about our ability to absorb the most tragic of events or otherwise confabulate their existence entirely?

Either way, it doesn't matter: my Nanny was dying and I can't really remember her decline and maybe that's a blessing. Of course, I have information from my family that, much like the children of the 2004 Tsunami, were able to fill in some gaps but I myself physically unable recall specific moments that I'm told happened. For example, my memory of seeing my Nanny with a bob and not her Jennifer Rush bouffant and then running around and out of the hospice she was in is so vivid to me now but might be entirely constructed or confabulated to fit with the observer narrative of my parents. Either way, none of that matters: my hero was fading away and my body protected me from it; of this I have no doubt.

I find it odd though, that I should start (and continue to) receive flashbacks of these 'forgotten' moments as I hit my 30s and beyond. So, as a teacher working with bereaved children, I'm forced to face my own prejudices of grief: what do we remember and why do we remember it?

If our first reaction to trauma as a mechanism of memory is an indicator of our ability to adapt (Norton, 2004) then I'm not okay. Picture the scene: we know Nanny is in a hospice and unwell and we are, this day, off to a theme park, American Adventure I think. We pack our bags early in the morning and the landline rings. Mom answers in a way that belies her Black Country upbringing but staggers. Within no time at all, it's clear the plans are changing and we – the kids – are whisked off to a safe place to watch films and be distracted. I'm the eldest of four ... I knew something wasn't right. My ten-year-old memory tells me it was 11:50 am when the call came that cancelled the theme park trip. But that was it for the moment until we returned home. We went into the kitchen where Mom told us Nanny had died. We all screamed in tandem and I've no idea how my Mom and Dad coped in this moment where their children exploded with explicit and visceral grief. We cannot ever, as teachers and educators, underestimate the deep and damaging effect this has on our students; not even empathy works here. To the absolute credit of my parents, we had grief counsellors on standby and were seen within days. The work was hugely helpful but I cannot remember engaging beyond a point and I still cannot remember in whole or part, the last few months of my Nanny's life.

As educators we need to be aware that these stories aren't fictional case studies for the betterment of a book but the real lived experience of people whose grief has shaped their entire lives. As a result, I find myself working with bereaved young people in an entirely different way that teachers with experience of adverse childhood experiences might otherwise do.

As identified by Cohen and Mannarino (2011) our priorities for grieving children could be:

1. Identify Child Grief Trauma (CTG) symptoms in educational environments.
2. Refer children for mental health assessments when necessary.
3. Recognise triggers that provoke trauma symptoms and find ways to manage these in schools.
4. Support CTG treatments by encouraging children's use of stress-management techniques.

However, let's not shy away from the truth: as schools, we are - more often than not - wholly ill-equipped to look after young children who need prescribed psychological systems of emotional repair. Our services are stretched beyond capacity, and our care workers cling to the crumbling system around them whilst referrals are triaged to the point that urgent and point-of-need care is completely unavailable.

If we cannot control these outside variables, then I suggest that we should start with a child-first approach, drawing on our collective sense of empathy and lived experience to provide:

- Time: with no-one being able to agree on suitable time periods for such traumatic experiences, we should be allowing our young people the time they need to process. We can do this in school by being actively aware of their reactions to everyday events and ensuring that their class teacher and support staff are also alert to sudden changes. No sense of urgency or rushing should be placed on them to talk about their experiences or feelings.
- Space: similarly, all responsible adults should be allowing for enough physical space around the child. Are they being coddled by friends or, conversely, being given too much space if social relationships are breaking down or not overly strong.

Gentle interventions can take place with a trusted friend with their class teacher to help the child articulate their wishes: they may well wish to be left alone. In this instance, a safe space should be available for them to feel a sense of psychological safety. Your school may well now be their 'safe space' away from the trauma of home and so it's important that we have the space to make this a reality if it's needed.

- Language: Taking the time to identify the triggers (Cohen and Mannarino, 2011) will likely necessitate your own research into common themes and words of grief and aligning this with your own understanding and knowledge of the child. As with our safeguarding duties, open questions can be used to ascertain mood and current emotions that are fuelling actions and behaviours in school. A mixture of positive and neutral language will help facilitate gentle conversations, especially if the class teacher is not experienced in this particular area.

When our children spend six hours per weekday in school, their class teacher and supporting adults become a de facto support network that must, somehow, navigate the myriad complexities of childhood grief. Support from our institutions isn't arriving any time soon and so we must look to these accidental caregivers to use their humanity, empathy and loved-experiences to support the most vulnerable of our young people. In the absence of services and professional support, class teachers should look to their knowledge of the child in front of them and start there: child first.

## Conclusion

The ways in which we grieve vary and are not a clear linear path. For practitioners and teaching staff helping children and young people as they negotiate their own grief journeys, this can make support more challenging, as the emotions are complex and varied. Looking at different models can help us understand some of the phases and stages of grief cycles.

Self-reflection questions to encourage deeper thinking:

- **Which grief cycle or grief theory resonated with you in this chapter?**
- **What are some ways we can support children on their grief journeys?**
- **How do you now understand the terms 'grief' and 'bereavement'?**

## Bibliography

Arizmendi, B.J. and O'Connor, M.F. (2015). What is "normal" in grief?. *Australian Critical Care*, 28(2), 58-62.
Bonanno, G.A. (2009). *The Other Side of Sadness: What the New Science of Bereavement Tells Us about Life after Loss*. Basic Books.
Cohen, J.A. and Mannarino, A.P. (2011). Supporting children with traumatic grief: What educators need to know. *School Psychology International*, 32(2), 117-131. https://doi.org/10.1177/0143034311400827.
Cronin Favazza, P. and Munson, L.J. (2010). Loss and grief in young children. *Young Exceptional Children*, 13(2), 86-99.
Dawson, K.S. and Bryant, R.A. (2016). Children's vantage point of recalling traumatic events. *PLoS One*, 11(9), e0162030. https://doi.org/10.1371/journal.pone.0162030.

Di Giuseppe, M., Prout, T.A., Ammar, L., Kui, T. and Conversano, C. (2021). Assessing children's defense mechanisms with the Defense Mechanisms Rating Scales Q-sort for Children. *Research in Psychotherapy*, 24(3), 590. https://doi.org/10.4081/ripppo.2021.590.

Frei-Landau, R. (2023). Who should support grieving children in school? Applying Winnicott's viewpoint to conceptualize the dyadic roles of teachers and school mental-health professionals in the context of pediatric grief. *Frontiers in Psychiatry*, 14, 1290967. https://doi.org/10.3389/fpsyt.2023.1290967.

Holland, J. (2008). How schools can support children who experience loss and death. *British Journal of Guidance & Counselling*, 36(4), 411-424.

Kastelnik, M. (2024). Prolonged grief: The predictive value of cognitive distortions, depression, and anxiety. PCOM Psychology Dissertations, 659. Available at: https://digitalcommons.pcom.edu/psychology_dissertations/659.

Klass, D., Silverman, P.R. and Nickman, S.L. (Eds.). (1996). *Continuing Bonds: New Understandings of Grief*. Taylor & Francis.

Kübler-Ross, E. (1969). *On Death and Dying* (1st ed.). Routledge. https://doi.org/10.4324/9780203010495.

Norton, G.R. (2004). Remembering trauma. Richard McNally. Cambridge, MA: Belknap Harvard, 2003. 416 Pages. ISBN 0-674-01082-5. *Cognitive Behaviour Therapy*, 33(2), 112-112.

Parkes, C.M. (1998). Coping with loss: Bereavement in adult life. *BMJ*, 316(7134), 856-859. https://doi.org/10.1136/bmj.316.7134.856.

Pomeroy, E.C., Garcia, R.B., Pomeroy, E.C. and Garcia, R.B. (2011). Theories of Grief and Loss: An Overview. In E.C. Pomeroy and R.B. Garcia (Eds.), *Children and Loss: A Practical Handbook for Professionals* (pp.1-16). Oxford University Press.

Stroebe, M. and Schut, H. (1999). The dual process model of coping with bereavement: Rationale and description. *Death Studies*, 23(3), 197-224. https://doi.org/10.1080/074811899201046.

# 5 How children understand death

- What is your own understanding of death?
- Are you aware of different ways that children process loss?
- How do you acknowledge grief in your classroom?

## Introduction

Understanding death is a complex process that varies significantly across different developmental stages. For children, the concept of death evolves as they grow, influenced by their cognitive, emotional, and social development. This chapter explores how children comprehend death at various ages, providing insights into their unique perspectives and reactions. Although this book is focussed on primary schools, I have included up to 18 to give an insight of what your pupils siblings may be going through. Additionally, it addresses the specific needs of children with Special Educational Needs and Disabilities (SEND) and those who are neurodiverse, acknowledging that these children may require tailored support to process and cope with loss.

Children with SEND and neurodiverse conditions, such as autism and ADHD, often have distinct ways of understanding and reacting to death. Their cognitive and emotional frameworks necessitate specialised approaches to help them navigate bereavement effectively. Understanding these unique needs is crucial for providing appropriate support that respects their developmental and individual differences.

Moreover, supporting children through the process of understanding death and coping with grief is not limited to the bereaved child alone. The entire class community can be affected by loss, necessitating a comprehensive approach to bereavement management within the educational setting. This chapter will also discuss strategies for whole class management, emphasising the importance of creating a supportive and understanding environment for all students.

By examining the varied ways children understand death and the specific needs of those with SEND and neurodiverse conditions, this chapter aims to equip adults: parents, carers and guardians, educators and caregivers, with the knowledge and tools to provide stage- and age-appropriate support. Through clear communication, emotional reassurance and structured support systems, adults can help children navigate the difficult terrain of grief and loss, fostering resilience and emotional well-being.

DOI: 10.4324/9781003532088-5

## How children understand death at different ages

### *Infants and toddlers (0-2 years)*

Before infants develop object permanence, which occurs in the second half of their first year, they cannot comprehend a permanent loss. Object permanence typically develops between 6 and 12 months of age and marks a crucial cognitive milestone where infants realise that objects and people continue to exist even when out of sight. As object permanence develops, infants begin to grasp that objects and people still exist even when not visible. This lays the foundation for understanding separation and loss. This development often aligns with the emergence of the game peek-a-boo; in this game children show concern at separation and joy at reunion, as if they are 'playing' with the idea of loss. Infants who do not understand death are highly attuned to the emotional states of their caregivers and can pick up on distress, even if they don't understand the reasons behind it. When a primary caregiver is absent or emotionally distressed, infants may become more irritable, crying more frequently or being harder to soothe. Disruption in the caregiver's presence or emotional state can lead to altered sleeping patterns, such as frequent night wakings or difficulty falling asleep. Infants may also eat less or refuse food when they sense a significant change in their environment or caregiver's emotional state.

### *Preschoolers (3-5 years)*

Preschoolers often see death as temporary and reversible, a belief reinforced by cartoons and fairy tales. Preschoolers may repeatedly ask about the deceased person. This repetition is their way of processing and making sense of the concept of death, for example, a child might frequently ask, 'When is Grandma coming back?' or 'Can we visit Grandpa now?'

Stress and confusion about death can cause preschoolers to revert to earlier stages of development, for example, a child who has been potty-trained might start wetting the bed again or a child might return to thumb-sucking or other comfort behaviours they had outgrown. Preschoolers often incorporate themes of death into their play as a way to explore and understand the concept, such as playing 'funeral' with their toys and acting out the roles of people at a funeral service. They might also play games where a character dies and then comes back to life, reflecting their belief in the reversibility of death.

### *Primary and junior school age (6-9 years)*

Children begin to understand that death is final but may believe it only happens to others and not themselves or their family. Knowing something is different from accepting it. Children at this stage know that death is a permanent state. They understand that once someone dies, they do not come back; however, accepting the finality of death, especially in relation to themselves or loved ones, can be more challenging. This acceptance process can be slow and may involve various emotional reactions. Children of this age might worry about what happens to the deceased after death. They may have concerns about the deceased's comfort or situation, for example, 'Is Grandpa cold in the ground?' The realisation of death's finality can lead to anxiety, particularly about their own mortality or the potential death of other loved ones. Children may become fearful about sleeping or being alone, worrying that something might happen to them or their family. Emotional distress about death can manifest as physical complaints such as stomach aches, headaches or other unexplained pains.

### *Pre-teens (10-12 years)*

Pre-teens understand that death is final and inevitable, and it can happen to anyone, including themselves and their loved ones. Pre-teens may feel deep sadness and sorrow about the loss of a loved one. Anger can be directed at themselves, others or even the deceased for leaving them. They may also become fearful about their own mortality or the potential death of other family members.

They might withdraw from family and friends, seeking solitude as they process their emotions; some may exhibit anger through rebellious or defiant behaviour as a way of expressing their inner turmoil. Children of this age may develop an acute awareness of their own mortality, leading to anxiety and preoccupation with the idea of death and worry about the health and safety of family members and friends.

### *Teenagers (13-18 years)*

Teenagers have an adult-like understanding of death, including its permanence. However, although they have a mature conceptual understanding of death, they still experience challenges adjusting to the death of someone. Teenagers might struggle with profound questions about the meaning of life and death, their own mortality and the purpose of existence. They may ask things like 'What happens after we die?' or 'What's the point of living if we all die anyway?' As a result, some teenagers might engage in risky behaviours, as a way to cope with or escape the intense emotions related to grief. This can include substance abuse, reckless driving or other dangerous activities. They may exhibit signs of depression, including persistent sadness, loss of interest in activities and changes in sleep and appetite. Anxiety might manifest as excessive worry, restlessness and physical symptoms like headaches or stomach aches. They might have panic attacks, be overly concerned about safety or display obsessive behaviours.

## Children's feelings of guilt about death

Children may experience feelings of guilt or believe that a death is their fault under certain circumstances. This typically happens when their understanding of cause and effect is not fully developed or when they are unable to rationalise events outside their control.

At age 3-6 years, children are very egocentric, meaning they see the world from their own perspective. They may believe that their thoughts, wishes or behaviours caused the death.

Between ages of 6 and 9 children often engage in magical thinking. They might believe that their thoughts or actions have power over real-world events. Ages 9-12 develop concrete operational thinking and start to understand more complex ideas, but they may still struggle with abstract concepts. They might link unrelated events logically but incorrectly. For example, they might think, 'If only I had been there to help, this wouldn't have happened'.

Teenagers can understand the complexities of life and death, but they might still feel guilt, especially if they had a conflicted relationship with the deceased or were involved in the situation leading to the death. For example, a teenager might feel responsible for a friend's death if they were present during an accident or if they didn't prevent risky behaviour.

There are also situational factors. Children who were present during the death or who witnessed traumatic events leading to the death may feel responsible. Children who do not fully understand what caused the death might fill in gaps with their own explanations, often leading to self-blame, for example, a child who is not given a clear explanation about a grandparent's death might assume it was because they didn't visit often enough.

## Supporting children to understand death at different ages

Supporting children through bereavement and grief requires age-appropriate approaches tailored to their developmental stages. There is a section towards the end of this book that will provide you with specific resources and ideas.

### *Infants and toddlers (0-2 years)*

- Maintain regular routines to provide a sense of security.
- Offer extra hugs, cuddles and physical closeness.
- Use simple language to explain the absence of a loved one, e.g., 'Grandma is not here, and we are sad'.
- Use a calm tone to reassure them.
- To ease separation anxiety, caregivers can practice gradual separations, starting with short periods and gradually increasing the time apart, helping infants adapt to the concept of temporary absence.

### *Preschoolers (3-5 years)*

- Use concrete language, avoid euphemisms. Explain that death means the body stops working and cannot come back.
- Reassure them that they are safe and taken care of.
- Encourage them to express their feelings through play, drawing or talking.

### *Primary and junior school age (6-9 years)*

- Answer questions honestly and provide clear information about death.
- Encourage them to express their emotions and validate their feelings.
- Engage in activities like drawing pictures, writing letters or creating memory boxes to remember the deceased.

### *Pre-teens (10-12 years)*

- Have open, honest conversations about death and encourage them to ask questions.
- Maintain open communication, allowing them to ask questions and express concerns.
- Encourage interactions with friends and peer support groups.
- Involve them in memorial services or other rituals to help them process their grief.

### Teenagers (13-18 years)

- Be available to listen without judgement and provide emotional support.
- Signpost to counselling or support groups
- Encourage healthy ways to cope, such as sports, arts or writing.
- Respect their need for independence and privacy while being available for support.
- Encourage them to talk about their feelings and seek help if they need it.

## How children with SEND and neurodiversity understand death

Children with SEND and neurodiversity (such as autism, ADHD and other developmental differences) can have unique ways of understanding and processing the concept of death. Their comprehension and reactions can be influenced by their cognitive, emotional and communication abilities. They can be particularly vulnerable when dealing with bereavement and understanding death. Their unique needs and challenges require tailored approaches to support their emotional and cognitive processing of such significant events. Changes in routine and the emotional responses of others can increase anxiety and confusion. They may struggle to articulate their feelings, leading to frustration or behavioural issues. Some children may exhibit regressive behaviours, such as bedwetting or tantrums, as a response to stress and grief. Grief may manifest as aggression, withdrawal or other challenging behaviours due to their difficulty in processing emotions. The emotional upheaval and changes in environment or routine may overwhelm children with SEND, leading to increased sensitivity or shutdowns. They might not pick up on social cues related to mourning and may appear insensitive or confused by others' reactions.

## Children with Autism Spectrum Condition

Children with Autism Spectrum Condition (ASC) might have a literal and concrete understanding of death. They may struggle with abstract concepts like the permanence of death. They may show repetitive questioning about the death, difficulties in expressing emotions, and might exhibit changes in behaviour or routines.

## Children with ADHD

Children with ADHD may understand death similarly to neurotypical peers but might have difficulty focussing on and processing information about death. They might exhibit impulsive reactions, difficulty in maintaining attention during discussions about death, and show behavioural changes like increased hyperactivity or distractibility.

## Children with learning difficulties

The level of understanding can vary widely depending on the severity of the disability. Some may understand death in a concrete way, while others may struggle with the concept entirely. They might exhibit a range of emotional responses, from apparent indifference to significant distress, and may have difficulty expressing their feelings verbally.

## Children with sensory processing disorders

These children might have typical cognitive understanding but can be overwhelmed by the sensory aspects of grieving environments (e.g., crowded funerals and loud noises). They might show sensory overload responses, such as withdrawal, agitation or meltdowns.

## Strategies for support

- Use simple, direct language and visual supports.
- Maintain regular routines to provide a sense of security and predictability.
- Validate their feelings, provide reassurance and be patient with their unique ways of expressing grief.
- Avoid using euphemisms, especially with children who have special educational needs or are neurodiverse. Phrases such as 'She will always be watching over you', 'He will always be in your heart' or 'They have gone to sleep forever' can cause anxiety, as these literal interpretations may lead to fears about being watched, sleeping or the confusing idea of why a person who was once living now resides in their heart. It's crucial to use clear, honest communication to reduce unnecessary distress.
- Seek guidance from psychologists, counsellors or therapists who specialise in working with neurodiverse children.

## The whole classroom

The realisation that death can happen can profoundly impact children in various ways. Understanding and addressing these impacts in a classroom setting is crucial for supporting all pupils effectively.

## Emotional reactions

Children may develop fears about their own mortality or the potential loss of other loved ones. This anxiety can manifest as difficulty sleeping, separation anxiety or heightened worries about safety. Witnessing a classmate's grief can evoke feelings of sadness and empathy. Children might feel deeply for their grieving peers and reflect on their own experiences with loss. Younger children may struggle to understand the concept of death. This can lead to confusion and a lot of questions as they try to make sense of what it means for someone to die.

## Behavioural changes

Some children may act out their confusion and fear through disruptive behaviour, while others may withdraw and become quiet and introspective. Children might become more attached to their caregivers, seeking reassurance and comfort. The emotional upheaval can make it difficult for children to focus on schoolwork, leading to a temporary decline in academic performance.

## Social dynamics

The class might rally around the grieving child, offering support and kindness. This can foster a sense of empathy and compassion among students. Alternatively, the grieving child may feel isolated if their peers are unsure how to offer support or if they inadvertently say things that are hurtful or insensitive. Themes of death and loss may emerge in children's play and conversations as they process their understanding of what has happened.

## Cognitive development

The death of a classmate's loved one can prompt children to confront the permanence of death, a concept that develops gradually. This can be a significant moment in their cognitive and emotional growth. Older children and pre-teens may begin to ask deeper, existential questions about life and death, the afterlife and the meaning of existence.

## Strategies for supporting the whole class

- Inform the class and provide an age-appropriate explanation about what has happened.
- Facilitate open, honest discussions about death, tailored to the developmental level of the students. Encourage questions and provide clear, age-appropriate answers.
- Let children know that it's okay to feel a range of emotions and that everyone grieves in their own way. Reinforce that their feelings are valid.
- Encourage classmates to support the bereaved child.
- Reassure children about their safety and the safety of their loved ones. Reinforce that while death is a part of life, most people live long, healthy lives.
- Provide various outlets for children to express their feelings, such as art, writing or talking. Group activities that promote sharing and empathy can also be beneficial.
- Keeping a consistent routine can provide a sense of normalcy and security for children amidst the confusion and disruption of grief.
- School counsellors and psychologists can offer additional support and strategies for helping children cope with their emotions.
- Acknowledge and respect cultural differences in how families and communities handle death and grieving. This can help children feel understood and respected in their diverse experiences.
- Include activities that allow for expression, such as art or storytelling; for more on this see Chapter 14.
- Monitor reactions and observe behaviours. Pay attention to changes in behaviour or mood among all students.
- Offer additional support to those who seem particularly affected. Chapter 14 signposts to a number of external organisations who may be of use.

## Conclusion

In conclusion, understanding how children perceive death at different developmental stages, including those with SEND and neurodivergence, is crucial for providing effective support.

By recognising the unique ways children process loss and tailoring approaches to their cognitive and emotional needs, adults can foster a supportive environment that promotes resilience and emotional well-being. Through clear communication, empathy and structured support systems, we can help children navigate the complexities of grief, ensuring they feel safe, heard and understood.

Self-reflection questions to encourage deeper thinking:

- **How has my own understanding of death evolved over time, and how might that influence the way I support children experiencing grief?**
- **Am I prepared to recognise and respond to the diverse ways children, including those with SEND and neurodiverse conditions, process loss? What strategies could I improve or adopt?**
- **How can I create a supportive classroom environment that acknowledges grief while ensuring all children feel safe, heard and understood?**

## Bibliography

Autism Speaks. (n.d.). *Grief and bereavement resources for people with autism*. [online] Available at: https://www.autismspeaks.org/grief-and-bereavement-resources.

Child Bereavement UK. (2019). *Child Bereavement UK*. [online] Available at: https://www.childbereavementuk.org/.

Child Bereavement UK. (n.d.). *Supporting a bereaved autistic child*. [online] Available at: https://www.childbereavementuk.org/supporting-a-bereaved-child-who-is-autistic#:~:text=Use%20simple%2C%20concrete%20language%20and.

Child Mind Institute. (2024). *Helping children cope with grief*. [online] Available at: https://childmind.org/guide/helping-children-cope-with-grief/#:~:text=Don (Accessed: 6 August 2024).

Dougy Center. (n.d.). *Grief support for parents & caregivers*. [online] Available at: https://www.dougy.org/grief-support-resources/parents-caregivers.

HealthyChildren.org. (2024). *How children understand death: What to say when a loved one dies*. [online] Available at: https://www.healthychildren.org/English/healthy-living/emotional-wellness/Building-Resilience/Pages/How-Children-Understand-Death-What-You-Should-Say.aspx#:~:text=School%2Dage%20children&text=Knowing%20something%20is%20different%20from (Accessed: 6 August 2024).

Lissienko, K. (2011). *Bereavement reactions of children & young people by age group*. [online] KidsHealth NZ. Available at: https://www.kidshealth.org.nz/bereavement-reactions-children-young-people-age-group#:~:text=Children%20increasingly%20become%20aware%20that.

Mencap. (n.d.). *Dealing with a bereavement*. [online] Available at: https://www.mencap.org.uk/advice-and-support/wellbeing/dealing-bereavement.

National Association of School Psychologists (NASP). (n.d.). *Addressing grief*. [online] Available at: https://www.nasponline.org/resources-and-publications/resources-and-podcasts/school-safety-and-crisis/mental-health-resources/addressing-grief.

Salek, E. and Ginsburg, K. (2019). *How children understand death & what you should say*. [online] HealthyChildren.org. Available at: https://www.healthychildren.org/English/healthy-living/emotional-wellness/Building-Resilience/Pages/How-Children-Understand-Death-What-You-Should-Say.aspx.

Schonfeld, D.J. and Demaria, T. (2016). Supporting the grieving child and family. *Pediatrics*, 138(3), e20162147–e20162147. https://doi.org/10.1542/peds.2016-2147.

www.autism.org.uk. (n.d.). *Bereavement*. [online] Available at: https://www.autism.org.uk/advice-and-guidance/topics/mental-health/bereavement.

# 6 Different perspectives on death and the afterlife

- How do those from different religions and those with no religion view death?
- Do all religions and belief systems agree that there is an afterlife?
- How might this influence the grieving process?

## Introduction

As we touched upon earlier in this book, experiences of faith can impact on a person's bereavement journey. In times of loss for those families and individuals who follow a particular faith or belief system it can be a great comfort, though conversely losses can also cause people to question their faith, as they struggle to make sense of the death. As we have reiterated throughout this text, the way people experience death of a loved one is unique and the individual is the expert. It is very important not to impress upon a child your own beliefs on death or an afterlife but to be respectful of theirs. We cannot know to what extent their faith is a comfort or a challenge under the circumstances, unless we are told.

As the school adult supporting the bereaved child this chapter provides an overview of the major world religion's views and a humanist view of death and grief which will give you some awareness of the teachings the child may have received from their beliefs, surrounding death.

> This chapter has been written with input from Paddy Hudspith, an experienced educator, trainer and writer, specialising in the intersection of religions, worldviews, philosophy and culture. He is currently Head of Religions & Ethics at Pilton Community College, Devon.

## Christianity

### Understanding of death

Christians believe that whilst we all die and our human body comes to an end, this is not **the** end. In the Bible Jesus reassures Mary that 'I am the resurrection and the life. Those who believe in me, even though they die, will live…' (John 11:25). Christians believe they too can be raised from death and share Jesus' risen life in heaven with others who have made the same journey.

### What happens to the deceased after death including belief in the 'afterlife'

Medical staff, carers or family wash the body and dress the deceased (usually in smart clothes), then they are collected by an undertaker who prepares the body to give a pre-mortem appearance both for the dignity of the deceased and for the families who may choose to view their loved one prior to burial. This may or may not include embalming, this is a choice made by the family and the purpose is to preserve the body for longer. The deceased is then dressed in their best clothes before being placed in the coffin of the family's choice with hands placed in a crossed position on their chest. At the heart of Christianity is the belief that God loves humanity so much that he gave his only Son, Jesus Christ, so that all those who freely choose for their sins to be forgiven because of Jesus's atoning sacrifice on the cross will be with God forever (Heaven), but those who freely reject God's offer of forgiveness of sin will be separated from God forever (Hell). Some believe this happens as soon as they die, others believe there is a period of waiting until a Day of Judgement. Christians believe that heaven is a place without pain or suffering, a place of endless love and peace and where God lives with his people beyond death. This promise of eternal life with God in Heaven gives Christians a hopeful perspective to contrast with any present sufferings they endure and the brute fact of physical death which awaits all humans.

### Mourning/grief/bereavement

Christians believe that God is with them through all the seasons of life including grief, and Christians will try to emulate Jesus himself at the tomb of his friend Lazarus, by 'weeping with those who weep' (Bible verse Romans 12:15) through pastoral care and concern.

## Islam

### Understanding of death

Muslims believe that when you understand death you do not need to be frightened by it even though we can't control when it happens. It is understood that Allah sends his angel 'Azrael' (the angel of death) to retrieve the soul from the human and once this happens you are declared dead (on Earth). 'Allah takes the souls at the time of their death'. 39:42, Holy Quran.

### What happens to the deceased after death including belief in the 'afterlife'

After the death the Muslim community alongside family conduct a ritual purification of the body followed by a funeral prayer and many other prayers, after which the body is buried. After sometime in the grave, Muslims believe that two angels 'Munkar' and 'Nakir' visit the deceased to test their faith, the result will be peaceful rest or punishment until either Allah is satisfied or the day of resurrection. 'Barzakh' is a period between a person's death and his resurrection. This waiting period is seen to be pleasurable or difficult depending on the strength of faith during the person's life. Muslims believe that when Allah decides this stage is over the day of resurrection will come and that the final resting place will be decided on judgement day, referring to how the person lived their life on Earth. Cremation is not permitted in Islam; the body must await resurrection from the grave and not be destroyed by fire.

*Different views of death and the afterlife* 41

*Mourning/grief/bereavement*

Muslims believe that death is a part of Allah's plan and this decision must not be questioned. It is permissible to express grief and to feel sad but this should not be excessive sadness as it is disrespectful to Allah. During the official mourning period of three days, the bereaved stay at home and food will be provided by relatives and friends.

## Hinduism

### Understanding of death

The central Hindu belief is that of reincarnation; when someone dies, the soul is reborn in a different form. This is in the context of samsara, the cycle of life, death and rebirth. This can happen multiple times, each incarnation aiming to live a better life, so as, at death, to achieve oneness with Brahma, the divine all-encompassing reality existing in and through all things. The soul's incarnation or form will depend on the actions of the previous life, known as 'Karma'.

### What happens to the deceased after death including belief in the 'afterlife'

Hindus believe that after death, the physical body is obsolete and cremation is the fastest way to release the soul and help with reincarnation. The eldest son of the bereaved or a Hindu priest oversees mantras or chants over the body. Other rituals include washing the body, placing essential oils on the head of the deceased and placing palms in a position of prayer and either wrapping the body in a white sheet or dressing them smartly. The cremation is usually within 24 hours of death, and until this time the body remains at the family home where family and friends visit to offer their sympathy to the bereaved. At a Hindu funeral guests are expected to view the body of the deceased in an open casket. A Hindu priest and senior family members conduct the cremation ceremony ('mukhagni'). Ashes are scattered over a place of importance to the deceased or a sacred body of water such as The Ganges, this is carried out a day after the funeral.

### Mourning/grief/bereavement

After the funeral and for 10-30 days it is a period of mourning, friends and family will likely visit and families may display a picture of their loved one with a garland of flowers. A 'preta-karma' ceremony is held on the 13th day of mourning to help release the soul for reincarnation and a memorial event a year after the death honours the life of the deceased.

## Buddhism

### Understanding of death

Buddhists generally believe that life and death are not distinctly separate, that the spirit continues after the body dies and that it may be reborn. Death therefore marks the end of one life and the transition into the next; it is just part of the cycle of birth, death and rebirth. According to the Buddha, beings go through numerous births and deaths until they gain enlightenment.

### What happens to the deceased after death including belief in the 'afterlife'

Prayer and meditation are important to Buddhists, and the spirit is enabled to leave the body correctly (via the head) in a calm and compassionate atmosphere as Buddhists believe that awareness after death may be retained for three days. The body must not be moved for at least four hours so that prayers can be said and when it is moved this should be done gently and with care. Bodies of Buddhists are not washed, only essential cleaning of excretions and touch is also limited. Cremation or burial takes place after a period of time and interment time varies across traditions. In most traditions prayers are said throughout the day and night and a 49 day prayer ritual in Tibetan practice is when the spirit moves through the afterlife and decisions surrounding rebirth are made.

### Mourning/grief/bereavement

Buddhists believe we have no choice but to be present with what is, in each moment, including grief. Buddhism teaches the individual to notice thoughts and feelings arising, let them go and return to the next new moment as it is now.

## Sikhism

### Understanding of death

Sikhs believe that death is part of life and a journey of the soul to re-join 'Waheguru' (the Sikh name for God).

### What happens to the deceased after death including belief in the 'afterlife'

Sikhism believes that the physical body is a 'shell' to house the soul and cremation is usually preferred. As a result of reincarnation, a belief that the soul of the deceased has moved to another body, there are no markers such as headstones, the ashes are more likely to be scattered over water or a significant place for that person. The funeral service is a celebration of the soul, and funeral arrangements begin no longer than three days after the person's death. Family members wash and dress the body and for those who are initiated (baptised) the five articles of Sikh faith, The Kangha (comb), The Kirpan knife, The Kara (bracelet), Kesh (uncut hair) and The Kachera (short-like undergarment), are left with the body. Orange and white chrysanthemums, the traditional mourning flower in many Asian countries, may be placed around the body by family members. Viewing the body depends on family customs.

### Mourning/grief/bereavement

Sikhs believe that mourning is a private affair and do not encourage public expression of emotion. Friends and family may gather in the Gurdwara to sing hymns and pray to mourn the loss and show God their acceptance of his decision to take their loved one. There is no official mourning period and no required rituals following the death of a loved one. However, starting on the day of death, the family read the entire 'Sri Guru Granth Sahib' the central holy religious scripture of Sikhism to comfort themselves in their grief. This may take three days if read continually or longer if it is not a continual reading.

## Judaism

### *Understanding of death*

In Judaism, death is accepted as a natural process and part of God's plan. Jews believe in an afterlife where those who have lived a good life in faith will be rewarded. However, descriptions and concepts are less clearly defined or universally upheld than in other faiths. Original Jewish scriptures spoke of an 'underworld' containing the souls of the dead which await a resurrection in 'the world to come', which is closely linked with an earthly future 'Messianic' era when a chosen leader will deliver the Jewish people from their enemies and establish an everlasting Kingdom of God over the whole earth.

### *What happens to the deceased after death including belief in the 'afterlife'*

After a person dies their eyes are closed and their body covered, candles are lit and 'guards' will sit with the body until the burial. The body is cleaned and wrapped in a simple shroud and buried in a simple coffin so that rich and poor receive equal honour in death. Open coffins are seen as disrespectful and not permitted. Bodies must be buried and not cremated and must come into contact with the earth because Jews believe the process of decay in the earth allows a gradual separation of the soul from the body which is more gentle than that of cremation.

### *Mourning/grief/bereavement*

On hearing of the death, the tradition is to tear your clothing, then recite a blessing to show acceptance of God's decision. Families express grief privately from the time of death to burial (usually one to two days). The next periods of mourning ('Shiva' for 7 days and 'Shloshim' for 30 days after the burial) limit comfort and pleasure, and clothes during Shiva are those worn at the funeral or on hearing the news 'Shloshim' is a little more pleasurable but music isn't listened to and there are no celebrations. 'Avelut' is similar, though it lasts for 12 months and is only for the death of a parent. Each anniversary of the death is acknowledged. Jews understand the mourning period to enable the mourner to fully express their grief. At the completion of the mourning period a tombstone is erected so the deceased will not be forgotten and the grave treated with respect.

## Humanism

### *Understanding of death*

Humanists are non-religious people who 'make sense of the world through logic, reason, and evidence' (Humanists.uk, 2025). A humanist is therefore an atheist (don't believe in God) or agnostic (don't believe it is possible to know for certain if a God exists). Humanists believe we are mortal, that we have just one life and many believe that acceptance of this can help us to live this one life more fully until the day we die. Death is the end of our individual existence.

### What happens to the deceased after death including belief in the 'afterlife'

A humanist funeral is non-religious and led by a celebrant. It celebrates the life of the deceased and may include readings, music (though these will be of a secular nature) and time for reflection. Humanists may be buried or cremated and their body or ashes interred in a crematorium, cemetery or green burial site or ashes scattered.

Although humanists do not believe in the afterlife, some believe that once our bodies break down, our atoms go on to form new things and our genes pass on to descendents if we have them. Also our actions, thoughts and ideas may live on through others and their memories of us and our written words, creations or societal contributions may also survive us; in other words our imprint on the world exists, even if we do not. Many people who are not humanists would also have these ideas as part of their religious or non-religious worldview.

### Mourning/grief/bereavement

Humanists acknowledge the pain of bereavement but focus on the life lived and memories shared in order to cope with the loss felt after a loved one dies. They acknowledge grief as a natural human reaction to the death of a loved one, an emotional response to stimulus.

## Conclusion

Every viewpoint accepts death as a fact, it will happen to us all. All of the major world religions emphasise that the nature of one's afterlife is determined, at least in part, by the choices one has made in life. 'Destinations' then become expressions of goodness and bliss, evil and torment, 'oneness with the Divine' or continued struggle/opportunity in the earthly world via reincarnation. Some non-religious world views believe your energy or soul continues for eternity in different guises.

All beliefs show the utmost respect for the deceased and the life they had, though some accept the body as a 'shell' or temporary 'housing' for the soul, and once the person is no longer breathing or their heart beating this shell is no longer of importance. Whilst the 'soul' is a widely held belief in most religions which continues beyond your physical existence, humanists believe that it is our connection with others through their memories of our lives and the impact we had on the world through our thought, words, actions or creations which lives on.

On a personal note I have found comfort in exploring the range of viewpoints in this chapter and whichever faith is followed or not, there is something of value in each belief to support the grieving process for every child. So long as the child clearly understands the person has died and they are not confused or frightened that the person is 'watching over them' or actually 'in their heart', if they find comfort in seeing a robin as a reminder of their loved one, for example, or a religious/non-religious act brings comfort this is helpful to the grieving process and the well-being of the child.

Self-reflection questions to encourage deeper thinking:

- **How do you think the view of death which the family holds may affect the thoughts and feelings the child may have or has already expressed?**
- **Does the family's belief provide comfort at this difficult time or could the family's previously held beliefs be challenged and how might this impact the child?**

## Bibliography

Buddhism for Beginners. (2022). *What do Buddhists believe happens after death?*. Available at: https://tricycle.org/beginners/buddhism/what-do-buddhists-believe-happens-after-death/ (Accessed: 22 February 2025).

Child bereavement UK. (no date). *Islam – death, dying and grief*. Available at: https://www.childbereavementuk.org/faqs/islam (Accessed: 18 February 2025).

Christian Evidence. (no date). *Life after death*. Available at: https://christianevidence.org/factfile/life_after_death/ (Accessed: 20 February 2025).

Christianity. (no date). *Life after death*. Available at: https://www.christianity.org.uk/article/life-after-death (Accessed: 20 February 2025).

Funeral Partners. (2024). *Hindu funeral rites and death rituals*. Available at: https://www.funeralpartners.co.uk/help-advice/arranging-a-funeral/types-of-funerals/hindu-funeral-rites-and-death-rituals/ (Accessed: 20 February 2025).

HSE. (no date). *Care of the dying – Buddhism*. Available at: https://www.hse.ie/eng/services/publications/socialinclusion/interculturalguide/buddhism/care-dying.html#:~:text=Generally%2C%20Buddhist%20teaching%20views%20life,of%20life%2C%20death%20and%20rebirth (Accessed: 22 February 2025).

Humanists UK. (no date). *Humanist funerals and memorials*. Available at: https://humanists.uk/ceremonies/non-religious-funerals/ (Accessed: 24 February 2025).

Humanists UK. (no date). *Think for yourself, ACT for everyone*. Available at: https://humanists.uk (Accessed: 19 February 2025).

Judaism 101 (JewFAQ). (no date). *Life, death and mourning*. Available at: https://www.jewfaq.org/death#Death (Accessed: 22 February 2025).

King James Version. (no date). *Bible gateway passage: John 11:25*. Available at: https://www.biblegateway.com/passage/?search=john+11%3A25&version=KJV (Accessed: 20 February 2025).

King James Version. (no date). *Bible gateway passage: Romans 12:15*. Available at: https://www.biblegateway.com/passage/?search=Romans+12%3A15&version=KJV (Accessed: 20 February 2025).

Lion's Roar. Available at: https://www.lionsroar.com (Accessed: 22 February 2025).

Muslim Aid. (no date). *What will happen after death according to Islam*. Available at: https://www.muslimaid.org/media-centre/blog/what-will-happen-after-death-according-to-islam/ (Accessed: 18 February 2025).

Rohatyn Jewish Heritage. (no date). *Jewish traditions for death, burial, and mourning*. Available at: https://rohatynjewishheritage.org/en/culture/death-burial-mourning (Accessed: 22 February 2025).

The Church of England. (no date). *Christian thinking on grief, bereavement and loss*. Available at: https://www.churchofengland.org/christian-thinking-grief-bereavement-and-loss (Accessed: 20 February 2025).

The Farewell Guide. (no date). *Sikh funeral rites – Your guide*. Available at: https://www.thefarewellguide.co.uk/sikh-funeral-rites (Accessed: 22 February 2025).

The Noble Qur'an. (no date). *Surat az-Zumar (the troops) – سورة الزمر*. Available at: https://legacy.quran.com/39/42 (Accessed: 23 February 2025).

Understanding Humanism. (no date). *What is Humanism?* Available at: https://understandinghumanism.org.uk/wp-content/uploads/2021/10/What-is-humanism-11.pdf (Accessed: 24 February 2025).

# 7 Childhood bereavement policy

- What is the purpose of a bereavement policy?
- What is meant by a 'childhood' bereavement policy?
- Key considerations for inclusion in the policy for support in the immediate aftermath of the death and in the long term.

## Introduction

> Death neither obeys the school timetable nor appears on it... it enters the classroom without knocking.
>
> (Winston's Wish, no date)

The death of a loved one is a devastating event for those directly involved and is also challenging for professionals such as teachers who are supporting vulnerable children without guidance. I speak from experience as a young teacher with about five years teaching experience but none supporting a bereaved child. I was lucky enough to be supported by a kind and knowledgeable governor who provided me with reading material and signposted me to a childhood bereavement charity 'See Saw' (no date) (see resources chapter for more information). However, as a busy teacher with day-to-day class management, supporting all children's social and emotional needs, preparing resources, teaching, providing feedback and making referrals to the bereavement charity, there was little time to read and digest the materials I was provided with. The intention for this book is for it to be an easy to navigate, quick read in times of crisis and a reference book to help settings 'be prepared and have plans in place to deal with death, grief and bereavement' (Child bereavement UK). This chapter highlights how important it is to identify the approach the school will take to supporting children in grief before a death has occurred, not in the often emotionally charged aftermath.

Death in the school community can be that of a:

- Grandparent
- Parent
- Sibling (either through miscarriage before birth or as a previously living child)
- Classmate/friend outside school
- A member of school staff
- A public figure

DOI: 10.4324/9781003532088-7

Each of these will affect the individual and the wider community in different ways and should be considered within a policy for 'childhood bereavement'. For a grandparent, parent or sibling the impact on one individual is the most likely outcome, though it should be borne in mind that other children are likely to be affected in some way as they recognise the topic of mortality and relate it to their own lives and families. If it is a member of staff or local community, some children may be more emotionally removed, though the death is likely to affect a larger number of children which will call for a different approach to that of an individual in a family, for example, when a member of staff died at our school, we set up a memorial garden which was open for anyone to have quiet time and reflect on the member of staff or indeed anyone in their own lives who had died.

The nature of death is also a crucial component affecting the bereaved:

- Life-limiting illness (which may have been witnessed over a long period of time)
- Sudden and unexplained death
- Death as a result of suicide
- Death as a result of homicide
- Death of a member of the military in military service

There is a difference between an expected death because the grief may have started long before the person died, and this can sometimes be called 'anticipatory grief' or 'living grief'; in my personal experience this doesn't lessen the pain after the person has died, it is just a prolonged grief and hard to understand your feelings prior to the death since the person is still with us; however, they are perhaps not the same as they once were and we mourn these changes from their physical appearance, strength and levels of activity to perhaps their change in mood.

A sudden and unexplained death will likely leave many unanswered questions as will that of a death by suicide which has the added complication that the person who has died made this conscious choice to end their life. It also often has a stigma attached to it largely due to historic reasons. In fact, suicide was punished as a crime in England and Wales until 1961, hence the term 'committed' suicide. Anyone who attempted suicide and survived could be prosecuted and imprisoned and for those who died, it was their families who faced the possibility of prosecution. It wasn't until the 1960s that a shift in thinking viewed suicide as an act of despair rather than criminality and a more supportive rather than punitive approach was encouraged, such as counselling, psychotherapy and suicide prevention intervention. Pitman et al. (2016) noted, 'Bereavement by suicide is a specific risk factor for suicide attempt among young, bereaved adults, whether related to the deceased or not'. Therefore, young people who have been bereaved by suicide need particular care and support for their own well-being.

A death through homicide is likely to have been sudden and violent and can have an impact on the wider community as well as those directly involved. There is likely to be additional distress in working with organisations such as the police, the media and the coroner and there may also be strong desire for justice. Due to the nature of the death some details are likely to be omitted when telling the child the person has died, whilst the information shared needs to be appropriate to the age and needs of the child, missing information can cause fear and confusion as the child tries to fill in the gaps. Seeing their family traumatised can be very upsetting as the people they usually turn to for support may well need additional support themselves. This is somewhat true of all grieving adults and their families, but the nature of homicide marks it out as uniquely distressing.

For those who have died whilst serving in the military, their families will likely face additional challenges. Their death may have been traumatic and yet prior to this they were a fit and healthy individual, there may be mixed or very strong feelings towards events resulting in the death and there could be a great deal of media interest to contend with. The family may have to relocate, leaving their military home which means moving away from their friends and 'military family' support network. If a parent or partner has died and you are a national from foreign or commonwealth countries the family may also now be affected by immigration laws. 'Standby' is a Military Bereavement in Education Project by Scotty's Little Soldiers, and a wealth of information can be found on their website such as the 'My Parent has Died' document with accompanying documents for educators. This is a very useful template for the child and surviving adult to complete providing key information for school. This has been specifically written for military families including information about which service they were in and whether or not the child is entitled to the service premium, but the contents of this form are a useful record of any child bereavement.

Given the profound statement at the start of this chapter, concerning death and its disregard to timetables or the common courtesy to knock, how can we be prepared to support a child who may experience a bereavement at any time? The starting point is to recognise that death, whether it be sudden, expected or through suicide is likely to impact us all at some point within our school communities. Having a policy will provide guidelines for staff in supporting children to navigate life after experiencing the death of a loved one or member of the school community. Does your school or Multi-Academy Trust have a bereavement policy? In particular, a childhood bereavement policy? I asked this in the straw poll via social media (Figure 7.1):

Figure 7.1 Screenshot of author's LinkedIn Survey asking 'Does your school have a bereavement policy?'

It is rather surprising don't you think that given death is a part of life and can happen at any time that less than half the respondents in the straw poll were aware that their school has a bereavement policy. The question did not identify whether this was a policy for staff or children. For staff this might include compassionate leave and supporting well-being with continued support perhaps through occupational health and for children there may be details of how and when death might be discussed throughout the curriculum, how we might support a child in the immediate aftermath of a death and what ongoing support might look like in the future. Child Bereavement UK states, 'A school or nursery with a bereavement policy is prepared and has plans in place to deal with death, grief and bereavement' (Child Bereavement UK, 2019).

Lytje et al. (2024) state that the type of grief experienced by bereaved children may depend heavily on the reactions and support from others and children may mirror how they see others reacting to the loss which may or may not be a healthy reaction. They suggest that resilience towards loss is built from 'appropriate and sensitive support from their community'. 'Their community' includes school, and whilst school staff know the children well, they identified that 'they often feel uncomfortable, unprepared, and unqualified to offer such support' (Dyregrov et al., 2013; Levkovich and Elyoseph, 2023); this can lead to avoidance and certainly discomfort for the adult, leaving the child without the support they need to cope. It is for this reason we are writing this book, to encourage you to be brave, to listen to the child and to offer them the 'appropriate and sensitive support'. A bereavement policy will provide a structure for what this support might look like and enable a setting-wide approach to be implemented and communicated to others.

If your setting does have a bereavement policy—well done, you are in the minority. When was it last updated? Does it reflect the current staffing structure and access to resources and groups which are still in operation? If you do not yet have one but are reflecting that it would be useful, there are several example policies available online and a suggested framework for a bereavement policy from organisations such as Childhood Bereavement UK and Winston's Wish. See our resource bank in Chapter 13 for other reference points. However as with any policy, it is important that it is appropriate for the organisation of your setting and reflects the organisation's ethos and values.

I had the pleasure of speaking with Martin Lytje from Denmark, a trained social educator, a doctor in education and a psychologist from the University of Bergen. His main research interests are within the areas of death studies, student voice and educational psychology. His work concentrates around providing professionals working with children the right tools to provide support during life crisis and bereavement. A study of his that interested me was an evaluation of bereavement response plans in Norway and Denmark (Lytje et al., 2021). It was interesting to note that the study found Norwegian plans, which were commercially produced, were of higher quality than the Danish plans, whereas the Danish plans, produced by the institutions themselves, were less impressive to look at, though arguably better tailored to the needs of the institution. If staff value the process, feel a part of it and it moves their thinking forward; they are more likely to find it a useful tool; plans need to benefit the staff in order to have a positive impact on the bereaved child. I was less interested in the comparison between countries and more interested in the fact that they exist and what is contained within them, though Martin and I agreed that the paperwork is less about the finished document, but more about the thinking process which institutions go through and rather than asking of a child's bereavement 'Do we have responsibility to support them?', we should ask 'WHAT IS our responsibility?'

I had been keen to look at these Bereavement Support Plans (BSPs) and to perhaps include an example in this book, but given that the document is less important than the thinking process I do not feel it is necessary. During our discussion I also learned that these plans are equivalent to a bereavement policy since I had misunderstood the BSPs to be individualised plans and Martin explained that it was more like a 'contract for how to manage bereavement'. What is fascinating is that these are not mandatory yet '87% of daycare facilities in Denmark and 98% in Norway' (Lytje et al., 2024) use these voluntarily and there has been a gradual increase in their use over the last seven years. When I asked Martin why he thought there was such a great uptake he replied simply, 'People see it works'. I followed this up by asking what he felt the impact of these plans had been on the children who had been bereaved. His response was confident 'It gives a sense of safety to staff who are not as worried in managing this type of event in the future and I've seldom met a child who has not been met at critical points'. By critical points Martin explained that the plans set out step by step what the school should do for the first four weeks after the death, such as making contact with the parents, carers and guardians to discuss amongst other details the funeral arrangements as well as perhaps commemorating the deceased in school. Martin recognised that the bereavement plans are not perfect, but they are a step in the right direction, he particularly noted that ongoing support in the aftermath of a bereavement and longer term still needs work.

His last comment about ongoing support led me to consider how we support individual students as they move through the school; how will each member of staff know a significant person in this child's life has died, perhaps a parent or a sibling, for example? Research highlights the death of a parent or sibling has been associated with 'potential vulnerabilities… These include challenges related to social interactions as well as mental and physical health' (McLaughlin et al., 2019). Emotional well-being of the individual could significantly impact their education which makes it even more important to note a significant bereavement and to communicate this with others throughout the child's school life. Many settings use software applications for monitoring child protection and pupil welfare, 'CPOMS' and 'TES My Concern' being two examples. These would appear to be the perfect tools to record a childhood bereavement. I contacted them both and a representative from CPOMS responded to say that it is something which could be added to the student's profile, by adding it to the 'Student overview' page via the summary; this would then be visible to any user who selects the student's profile. Alternatively, it can be recorded as an 'incident' which can then be pinned to the top of the student's profile making it appear at the top of the incident page. The bereavement could be recorded on your setting's chosen management information system such as SIMS, Arbor and Integris. If a template such as 'My Parent has died' on Scotty's Little Soldiers (no date) website is used this could be scanned in and attached to the child's school records. The recording of the bereavement is not instead of a school policy but one small element of it, a tool which supports the staff in identifying potentially difficult days in the child's life linked to their grief.

I would urge you to consider Figure 7.2 illustrating Stroebe and Schut's 'Dual Process Model' (1999) for a deeper understanding of bereavement in the longer term, such as a year or two after the death, and beyond.

*Childhood bereavement policy* 51

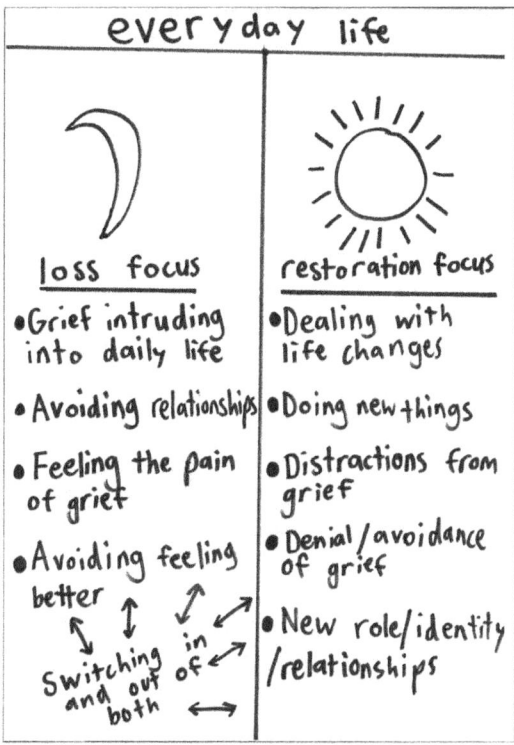

*Figure 7.2* Stroebe and Schut's 'Dual Process Model' (1999) drawn by James Watson aged 15

As referred to in Chapter 4, this model identifies two zones labelled 'loss' and 'restoration', demonstrating that a grieving individual moves back and forth between the two zones, illustrated by the term 'puddle jumping' in Chapter 2. To the casual observer the child may seem 'fine one minute and not the next'; perhaps they appear to be going 'backwards' if we misunderstand the stages of grief as linear. This can be a time of confusion for the grieving person as they may feel as though they are coping with 'normal life' and in another moment, be tearful or even swamped with difficult emotions where a simple task becomes an insurmountable challenge.

If at this point you are considering your setting's policy, a good starting point might be to explore the Winston's Wish Bereavement Charter since it is based on conversations with thousands of children and their families, who told the charity what gave them hope after bereavement. It can be found at: https://www.winstonswish.org/wp-content/uploads/2018/01/ww-0107-CBC-lo.pdf

Having established the importance of short-, medium- and long-term support and the benefits of a bereavement policy for children, I suggest below some key elements you may wish to include:

- Relationship with person who has died.
- When the person died, is it a recent or historic death?
- Immediate support for the individual and informing others as appropriate.

- How will the setting communicate with the family affected and the class of the affected student?
- Supportive network around the child: what is in place, is there anything missing? Will there need to be or have there been in the past, new living and care arrangements for the child?
- Nature of the death – expected/unexpected/military/suicide and how this can affect the child.
- Will a representative from school attend the funeral? Consider the family's wishes, they may want it to be a private affair, or they may appreciate someone from school attending.
- Supporting others in the class to manage their fear of someone in their own lives dying or triggering a past bereavement and guiding them to console the bereaved child in appropriate ways.
- Ongoing support throughout the child's school life noting that there is no timeline for grief and birthdays, anniversaries and significant days such as Mother's Day, Father's Day and religious festivals may trigger grief responses years from the initial trauma.
- An outline of the grief process especially in children, understanding the dual process model of Stroebe and Schutt 1999, whereby children (and adults) can move back and forth between loss focus and restoration focus as the bereaved person adapts to 'normal life' after loss.
- How will you be aware of historical bereavement and the long-term impact of the trauma, children who may arrive in school whose parent/close relative has already died and may still need support, rather than those who suffer a loss whilst at the school.
- Are there any Adverse Childhood Experiences alongside the bereavement?
- How to support a child with SEND in bereavement including those who are neurodivergent.
- Signposting to wider services.

Whilst few schools appear to have a policy in place for childhood bereavement, some of those that do are particularly well thought out and include headings such as:

Introduction, Rationale, Aims, Roles and responsibilities in dealing with bereavement
Procedures – Pre-bereavement, Following a bereavement (immediately, for the funeral, after the funeral and longer term)
Following a sudden and unexplained death – Suicide, Homicide
If A Child Dies in School/on a School Trip
Military Families
COVID-19
How to offer further support
Equality and inclusion, values and beliefs
Support for bereaved staff
Curriculum
Additional Support Links to charities and books on bereavement
Letter Templates

## Conclusion

There are some excellent examples of bereavement policies online and some superb frameworks available on the websites of childhood bereavement charities listed in the resources below. The key message is that it must be understood by your staff and supportive to your bereaved children; in summary it must work for your setting. You might find that a trust-wide policy is a great starting point but there should be flexibility within this to make it apply to each individual nursery/school.

Self-reflection questions to encourage deeper thinking:

- **Does your school have a 'Childhood' Bereavement Policy?**
- **Do you need to write one or update the one currently in place?**
- **What will you be sure to include?**
- **Where will you look for templates or ideas?**

## Bibliography

Child Bereavement UK. (2019). *Child bereavement UK.* [online] Available at: https://www.childbereavementuk.org/ (Accessed: 2 September 2024).

Cruse Bereavement Support. (2021). *What happens after a military death?* Available at: https://www.cruse.org.uk/organisations/grief-in-the-military/what-happens-military-death/ (Accessed: 3 January 2025).

Dyregrov, A., Dyregrov, K. and Idsoe T. (2013). Teachers' perceptions of their role facing children in grief. *Emotional and Behavioural Difficulties*, 18(2), 125–134. https://doi.org/10.1080/13632752.2012.754165

Glasgow Health and Social Care Partnership. (no date). *A whole school approach to loss and bereavement.* Available at: https://www.nhsggc.org.uk/media/270705/a-whole-school-approach-to-loss-and-bereavement-december-2021.pdf/ (Accessed: 4 January 2025).

Grief Encounter | Leeds bereavement forum. (no date). *Grief encounter.* Available at: https://www.griefencounter.org.uk (Accessed: 10 July 2024).

Holland, J. (2016). *Responding to Loss and Bereavement in Schools: A Training Resource to Assess, Evaluate and Improve the School Response.* Jessica Kingsley Publishers.

Levkovich, I. and Elyoseph, Z. (2023). "I don't know what to say": Teachers' perspectives on supporting bereaved students after the death of a parent. *OMEGA - Journal of Death and Dying*, 86(3), 945–965. https://doi.org/10.1177/0030222821993624.

Lytje, M., Dyregrov, A., Bergstrøm, M. D., Fjærestad, A. and Fisher-Hoyrem, L. (2021). Same origin, different implementations: A document analysis of Norwegian and danish bereavement response plans. *International Journal of Early Years Education*, 31(4), 1071–1085. https://doi.org/10.1080/09669760.2021.1902787.

Lytje, M., Dyregrov, A. and Gjestad, R. (2024). Evaluating bereavement response plans in daycare: A comparative analysis of support systems in Denmark and Norway. *Illness, Crisis & Loss*, 33(3), 702–716. https://doi.org/10.1177/10541373241268047.

McLaughlin, C., Lytje, M. and Holliday, C. (2019). *Consequences of childhood bereavement in the context of the British school system.* Available at: www.researchgate.net/publication/333866897 (Accessed on: 4 January 2025).

Pitman, A.L., Osborn, D.P.J., Rantell, K. and King, M.B. (2016). Bereavement by suicide as a risk factor for suicide attempt: A cross-sectional national UK-wide study of 3432 young bereaved adults. *BMJ Open*, 6(1). https://doi.org/10.1136/bmjopen-2015-009948.

Scotty's Little Soldiers. (no date). *Military bereavement in education.* Available at: https://www.scottyslittlesoldiers.co.uk/standby (Accessed: 10 July 2024).

See Saw. (no date). *Grief support for children and young people in Oxfordshire.* Available at: https://seesaw.org.uk/ (Accessed: 2 January 2025).

Stroebe, M. and Schut, H. (1999). The dual process model of coping with bereavement: Rationale and description. *Death Studies*, 23(3), 197–224. https://doi.org/10.1080/074811899201046.

Winston's Wish. (no date). Available at: https://www.winstonswish.org/ (Accessed: 2 January 2025).

# 8 What can we learn from special schools?

## Introduction

Special schools in the UK play a pivotal role in supporting bereaved children, particularly those who are neurodivergent, by tailoring their approaches to meet each child's unique needs. Recognising that neurodivergent children may express grief differently, special schools emphasise personalised support to help them navigate their emotions.

Research underscores the crucial role schools play in supporting bereaved children, including those with special educational needs (SEND). A review by Child Bereavement UK highlights that all children and young people, regardless of their circumstances, have a right to have their grief recognised, to hear the truth and to be given opportunities to express their feelings and emotions. Children and young people with learning difficulties are no different but may need extra help with their understanding and ways to express their feelings (Child Bereavement UK, 2024).

There can be a tendency to shield children with special educational needs and disabilities (SEND), particularly those with complex needs, under the belief that they are already coping with significant challenges. Every child who has experienced bereavement deserves the chance for their grief to be acknowledged and the space to express their feelings. During times of loss, they need compassion, understanding and support (Educators-barnardos.org.uk, 2024).

## Support needs

The loss of a loved one can be particularly challenging for children with SEND, who may respond differently to bereavement compared to their peers (Sudden, 2020). Children with SEND, including those with autism, often face difficulties in identifying and expressing their emotions. This can make the grieving process especially complex. For example, a bereaved child may recognise feelings of anger or sadness but struggle to articulate the reasons behind these emotions. In some cases, children may express emotions that seem inappropriate in the context of loss. A child might say they feel 'happy' about a bereavement, not because they are, but due to a lack of vocabulary to describe more complex feelings. Bereavement can create confusion, and the egocentric thinking common in childhood may lead some children to wrongly believe they are responsible for the death. This can result in heightened anxiety

DOI: 10.4324/9781003532088-8

and the formation of 'wrong connections'. For instance, a child whose loved one died in a car accident might develop an intense fear whenever a family member drives, associating vehicles with the risk of loss. Places or situations linked to the bereavement may also trigger distress. Change can be particularly overwhelming for individuals with SEND. The disruption caused by bereavement, such as altered routines, absence of familiar people or shifts in daily life, can trigger strong emotional reactions, including aggression or withdrawal. Children with SEND may initially focus on practical matters or routines, showing little outward sign of grief. Their emotional responses may emerge later once they've processed the immediate changes. Recognising this delayed grief response is essential to providing ongoing support tailored to their unique needs.

## Support strategies

Clear and concrete communication is essential, using simple language and visual aids to help children understand loss in a way that makes sense to them. Maintaining consistent routines provides stability and security, helping children feel grounded during this difficult time.

For children with SEND, as with very young children, maintaining consistent routines is vital, as it provides a sense of safety and stability during times of loss. It's also important to recognise that these children may express grief in unique ways, and educators, professionals and caregivers should accept and support these varied expressions.

Tailor support to individual needs and recognise that each child's experience of grief is unique. Personalise support strategies to align with the child's cognitive level, communication style and emotional needs, ensuring that interventions are both appropriate and effective.

Teaching emotional regulation strategies, such as sensory breaks, relaxation techniques and creative expression through art, music or storytelling, gives children healthy outlets to process their grief. Special schools also emphasise the importance of safe spaces where children can express their emotions at their own pace, fostering emotional healing in a supportive environment. Schools themselves can serve as safe spaces, offering a sense of normality and routine for bereaved children with SEND.

Involving parents, carers and guardians in the support process is crucial. Collaboration with families and therapists ensures a holistic approach, integrating professional guidance and parental support to provide the most effective care. A study focusing on bereavement during the COVID-19 pandemic emphasised the importance of family support and coping mechanisms in helping children navigate their grief (Harrop et al., 2022).

## Supporting children with life-limiting illnesses and disabilities

Supporting bereaved children with life-limiting illnesses and disabilities requires a nuanced approach that addresses their unique needs. For children with life-limiting illnesses, experiencing the death of someone close to them can bring an acute awareness of their own mortality. This realisation can be deeply distressing and complex, especially as they are already navigating the emotional and physical challenges of their own condition. However, how they process this awareness depends on several factors, including their age, cognitive development, emotional maturity and the support they receive from caregivers and professionals.

Children's understanding of death evolves with age as we explored in Chapter 5. Younger children may not fully grasp the permanence of death, while older children and adolescents are more likely to comprehend its finality, which can trigger existential questions about their own lives. Grieving a loved one while facing their own terminal illness can evoke feelings of fear, sadness, anger and anxiety. Some may internalise their fears, while others may openly express concerns about their own death, seeking reassurance from trusted adults. These children may experience anticipatory grief, which includes mourning their own future loss and the impact it will have on their families. This type of grief can coexist with mourning the death of someone else, compounding their emotional burden.

Research indicates that avoiding discussions about death can increase anxiety in children. Conversely, sensitive and honest conversations, tailored to the child's level of understanding, can alleviate fear and promote emotional well-being. Creating a safe space for children to express their feelings and ask difficult questions is essential (Arruda-Colli et al., 2017). Open communication with children who are dying is not merely about providing information but involves listening to the child's concerns and fears, thereby decreasing feelings of anxiety and allaying fears (The Health Psychologist, 2023).

## Supporting peers

Supporting students through the loss of a classmate requires a compassionate and structured approach that fosters understanding and healing. Encouraging open communication is essential, allowing students to express their feelings and ask questions about the loss in a safe and supportive environment. Providing honest, age-appropriate information helps demystify the situation and alleviate fears. Emotional support should also be readily available through counselling services or support groups, where pupils can share their experiences and find comfort in their peers. Maintaining routine and normalcy within the school setting offers a sense of stability, helping students navigate their grief while continuing their daily lives. Creating memorial activities, such as a memory wall or a commemorative event, can provide a meaningful way for classmates to honour their friend's life and find closure. Additionally, educating students about grief through structured programs reassures them that experiencing a range of emotions is normal and that seeking help is a sign of strength. You can find out more about supporting the whole school community in the next chapter with advice provided from a hospice.

## Learning from Special Schools

Special schools are indeed special places, filled with dedicated staff who understand the unique needs of children with disabilities and life-limiting illnesses. These environments are characterised by a profound sense of empathy, patience and tailored support, which creates a nurturing atmosphere for children facing significant challenges. Having worked in such environments, I can attest to the beauty and resilience found within these communities. The staff's commitment to understanding and addressing each child's unique needs fosters a sense of belonging and safety that is crucial for emotional and psychological well-being.

Special schools excel in recognising and responding to the diverse ways children with SEND express grief. These children may not always articulate their emotions verbally, but their behaviours and interactions often provide clues to their inner experiences. Staff in special schools are trained to observe and interpret these signals, offering support that is both sensitive and effective.

One of the key lessons from special schools is the importance of creating safe spaces where children feel secure enough to express their grief. These environments are designed to be predictable and comforting, with consistent routines that provide stability. This sense of safety is essential for bereaved children, as it helps them navigate their emotions without feeling overwhelmed.

Special schools emphasise personalised support, tailoring interventions to meet each child's cognitive and emotional needs. This approach ensures that support is appropriate and effective, helping children to process their grief in ways that make sense to them. Techniques such as clear communication, visual aids and sensory activities are commonly used to help children understand and express their feelings.

Children with SEND often have a unique ability to live in the moment, which can be particularly beneficial during times of grief. Special schools encourage present-focused activities that help children find joy and connection in their daily experiences. This approach teaches us the value of being present, providing comfort and stability during difficult times. By engaging in activities that promote mindfulness and immediate emotional expression, children can experience moments of relief and happiness, even amidst their grief.

Another crucial aspect of special schools is the collaborative approach to support. Involving families, caregivers and professionals ensures a holistic support system that addresses all aspects of a child's well-being. This collaboration is vital for bereaved children, as it integrates professional guidance with the emotional support of loved ones, creating a comprehensive network of care.

The resilience and compassion found within special schools are inspiring. Staff members are skilled not only in providing practical support but also in offering emotional comfort and understanding. This compassionate approach helps children feel valued and supported, fostering a sense of hope and healing.

Supporting staff in special schools is crucial due to the unique challenges they face. These educators often work with children who have complex needs, which can be emotionally and physically demanding. As a result, special schools typically have robust support systems in place for their staff, to better support them, and, in turn, bereaved children.

Special schools often provide ongoing professional development opportunities tailored to the specific needs of their staff. This includes training in specialised teaching methods, behaviour management strategies and emotional support techniques.

Recognising the high levels of stress and potential for burnout, special schools frequently offer access to counselling services, stress management workshops and peer support groups. These resources help staff manage their emotional well-being and maintain resilience.

Special schools foster a collaborative culture where staff can share experiences, strategies and support each other. Regular team meetings and collaborative planning sessions are common, ensuring that staff do not feel isolated in their roles.

Research highlights the importance of these support systems in preventing burnout and improving job satisfaction among special education staff. For example, a brief by EdResearch for Action discusses the persistent shortage of special education teachers and emphasises the need for administrative support and professional development to retain staff (Bettini and Gilmour, 2024). Another article from Edutopia outlines strategies for school leaders to uplift special education teachers and staff, including the importance of effective communication, collaborative problem-solving and creating a supportive school culture (Mitchell, 2025).

## Conclusion

By implementing these support measures, special schools create an environment where staff feel valued, supported and equipped to handle the unique challenges of their roles. This holistic approach ensures that educators are well-equipped to handle the emotional demands of their roles, ultimately leading to better support for students navigating grief. There are many lessons to be learned for other settings from a special school's approach.

Self-reflection questions to encourage deeper thinking:

- **How can I adapt my approach to supporting bereaved children with SEND, considering their unique ways of expressing grief and their need for clear communication and routines?**
- **In what ways can I collaborate more effectively with parents, carers, guardians and therapists to provide a holistic support system for bereaved children with life-limiting illnesses and disabilities?**
- **How can I create a compassionate and supportive environment for students who are grieving the loss of a classmate, while ensuring they feel comfortable expressing their emotions and accessing the support they need?**

## Bibliography

Arruda-Colli, M.N.F., Weaver, M.S. and Wiener, L. (2017). Communication about dying, death, and bereavement: A systematic review of children's literature. *Journal of Palliative Medicine, 20*(5), 548-559. https://doi.org/10.1089/jpm.2016.0494.

Bettini, E. and Gilmour, A. (2024). *Addressing special education staffing shortages: Strategies for schools – edresearch for action.* [online] EdResearch for Action. Available at: https://edresearchforaction.org/research-briefs/addressing-special-education-staffing-shortages-strategies-for-schools/.

Child Bereavement UK. (2024). *Supporting bereaved children and young people with a learning disability.* [online] Available at: https://www.childbereavementuk.org/supporting-bereaved-children-and-young-people-with-a-learning-disability (Accessed: 3 February 2025).

Educators-barnardos.org.uk. (2024). *Supporting bereaved children and young people with SEND.* Barnardos Education Hub. [online] Available at: https://www.educators-barnardos.org.uk/resources/b-a-supporting-bereaved-children-and-young-people-with-send (Accessed 3 February 2025).

Harrop, E., Goss, S., Longo, M., Seddon, K., Torrens-Burton, A., Sutton, E., Farnell, D.J., Penny, A., Nelson, A., Byrne, A. and Selman, L.E. (2022). Parental perspectives on the grief and support needs of children and young people bereaved during the COVID-19 pandemic: Qualitative findings from a national survey. *BMC Palliative Care, 21*(1), 177. https://doi.org/10.1186/s12904-022-01066-4.

Mitchell, K. (2025). *5 Interconnected ways for school leaders to uplift special education teachers and staff.* [online] Edutopia. Available at: https://www.edutopia.org/article/5-interconnected-ways-school-leaders-uplift-special-education-teachers-staff.

Sudden. (2020). *Supporting bereaved children with special educational needs - Sue McDermott and Katrina Avery - Sudden*. [online] Available at: https://sudden.org/tools/supporting-bereaved-children-with-special-educational-needs/ (Accessed 3 February 2025).

The Health Psychologist. (2023). *Communicating with the child dying of cancer: Professionals' attitudes, practices and observations*. [online] Society for Health Psychology. Available at: https://societyforhealthpsychology.org/read/the-health-psychologist/issues/2023-spring/ (Accessed 3 February 2025).

# 9 What can we learn from a hospice?

- What key lessons can we learn from hospice staff about supporting children with bereavement?
- How would you inform children, parents and staff of a death in the school community?

## Introduction

The NHS states, 'The aim of hospice care is to improve the lives of people who have an incurable illness' (NHS 14 April 2022).

Hospice care is probably best known for end-of-life care however, this is not the extent of the work they do, a hospice palliative care team might help to control symptoms of the person with the condition, such as pain, seizures, mobility or respiratory issues throughout their condition/illness, and they also support families and carers. They will therefore be acutely aware of the challenges families face throughout a life-limiting condition and it is very rare for a hospice to support the person with the condition without also supporting the family; one small aspect of this is respite for families so that the person with the condition/illness receives medical care required and the families have a period of time away from their caring role. Children's hospices often have accommodation, not just for the young person with medical needs but also for the family. A fun, supportive environment with craft activities, play and meals prepared is promoted, and 'sibs' teams support siblings throughout the condition/illness of their loved one, especially as many of them are young carers themselves, helping them to understand the journey they are on alongside their family, providing opportunities for questions to be answered and the chance for fun, laughter and simply enjoying childhood.

Shooting Star Children's Hospices are a leading children's hospice charity supporting over 700 children, and their families, throughout Surrey and across 14 boroughs of London. They run a specialist bereavement service, which allows families to access a personalised pathway of care. This support is for the whole family, for the first three years and three months after a child in the family has died. They have also worked with schools, advising them on bereavement support for children.

For this book, the Children's Psychological Therapies Team at Shooting Star Children's Hospices have written about communicating the death of a child to school communities, often the most difficult event for a school community. It is an invaluable distillation of therapists' knowledge through many years of talking with schools about bereavement. Whilst some aspects of this advice will apply specifically to the death of a child, much of it is sound advice which can be applied to communicating the death of any member of the school or wider community.

## Communicating with primary school communities where the death of a child has taken place – Children's Psychological Therapies Team at Shooting Star Children's Hospices

At Shooting Star Children's Hospices we are often approached by schools asking us how to tell their school community that a pupil has died. The death of a child causes ripples of sadness and shock across a school community. When this information is shared carefully and thoughtfully, it can help individuals support each other and grieve well.

### The family

- Begin by speaking with the family of the child to share your condolences and understand what information the family feels comfortable for you to share with others. Give them choice and control to determine the privacy they would like.
- Explain to them that the school community (staff and families) will undoubtedly wish to express their condolences and offer support. Find out if the family wishes to be contacted at this time or whether the school can help by collating these messages for them. Many families feel pressured to answer messages from other parents, carers and guardians, so reassure them that you are happy to collect their messages from the school community so they can receive these when they are ready.
- Explain that you will communicate with families of the school community in a letter and ask if they would like the opportunity to see this in the next few days, ahead of it being sent.
- If there are any siblings attending your school let the parents, carers and guardians know that you will be available to meet with them, to think about what support may be helpful.
- If media attention arises, ensure clear communication with the family about how to handle enquiries sensitively.

### Staff

- Take time to inform staff. Begin with the child's direct class teacher and teaching assistants. Share the news of the child's death in a one-to-one or small group setting. This can feel more supportive.
- Then bring all staff together. Share your sadness and some facts about the death (those you have permission to share). It is not uncommon for an unexpected death to set minds racing with questions about what happened.
- The death of the pupil may remind them of a recent or similar loss, and overwhelming feelings of grief can resurface. Let staff members know this might happen and encourage them to talk about this.

- The death of a pupil may create fear and anxiety about the well-being of their own child, children in their class or others they are close to. Encourage open conversations, empathise and offer support.
- If the death was unexpected or traumatic, staff members may experience disturbed sleep, increased anxiety, irritability or other symptoms. Explain that this is normal and it is important that they do not isolate themselves but talk to those around them.
- Everyone responds differently and that is okay. If staff experience the reactions described above, these are likely to subside over four to six weeks. If they do not, you might signpost staff members for further support.
- Think about ways you can give staff time and space to grieve. You may hold a special service, or create a book or online space to record condolences or memories. You don't have to have decided how you will do this at this stage. Encourage staff to think about how you as a school community would like to respond, and ask them to bring suggestions back to you.
- Allow staff to attend the funeral if invited and feasible.
- Assure staff that you will consider ways to provide training and guidance on supporting children with grief and bereavement to equip staff with strategies for their classroom.
- Staff may need extra one-to-one support and coaching at work, as they will be supporting children who have suddenly become bereaved of a friend, while also processing their own grief. Remind staff of the support systems you have available to them. Ensure support is in place for at least 12 months following the death of the child.

### Parents, carers and guardians of the school community

- It can be helpful to meet with parents, carers and guardians in the school community to tell them about the death. We find this is often impossible to do in a timely manner before families learn this information through other sources possibly including the media and social media, so we recommend emailing a letter to parents, carers and guardians as soon as you are ready to.
- Do not include details of the cause of death unless explicitly instructed by the family. This is confidential medical information that cannot be shared without permission from the child's parents, carers or guardians. It can be incredibly difficult to resist the call from other adults who are upset and anxious and feel that understanding the cause of death could bring them comfort, however the family has the right to keep these details private.
- Give families guidance on how to send condolences to the bereaved family (as agreed with the family).
- To ensure consistency, let parents, carers and guardians know when you will be talking to the children about the death and the wording and explanation you will use.
- Provide information on how to seek support for their child if they are struggling

with anxiety or grief. Talk about the symptoms. Explain how they can approach support structures within your school or via their general practitioner. Assure families that their child may experience acute feelings in the first few weeks. These may be about attachment, loss, anger, fear and sadness. Their behaviour may regress. They may notice their child is clingy and anxious about separation, is more easily angered or experiences nightmares, headaches and tummy aches. If these do not subside naturally, more professional support may be of help. Invite them to always be in communication with you as a school if their child is struggling.

### *Children in the school community*

- It is important that you inform the children in the school. If this is not done you cannot be sure as a school community that the same message is given to all children and 'playground whispers' can be troublesome.
- Meet with children in small groups at the same time; classes or tutor groups would usually work well.
    - Make sure you are in a comfortable space with minimal interruptions.
    - Let them know you have some very sad and important news to share with them.
    - Use the name of the child (make sure it is clear which child this is if there is more than one child with the same name in the school) and tell them that they have died.
    - We strongly advocate that adults use the word 'dead/died' when talking with children and young people to avoid confusion. If the children are younger, ensure they understand what dead and died means, including the permanency of this.
    - Do not use euphemisms like 'gone to sleep'. Instead, say that the child has died and explain this in age-appropriate terms. You might say that the child had an illness/accident. The doctors gave the child medicine/treatment, but they couldn't make them better. Their heart has stopped beating and their body has stopped working.
    - You can say that beliefs differ on what happens after somebody dies. However, when their body dies it cannot come back to life again and so they cannot come back to us which is what often makes us sad or angry.
    - Allow them to process this at their pace. Encourage questions and validate emotions. Some children may not react immediately but may have questions later. Provide opportunities for continued discussion. Remember that this is the beginning of a conversation and learning about experiencing the death of someone close.
    - Have a gentle activity the children can do afterwards, like colouring or journaling, to help them process their emotions.
    - Consider creating something together as a group to remember the child who has died, but this is something to do later in the day or week and not as soon

as they are told the news. Some examples are: creating a memory jar, drawing pictures of/for the child who has died, painting a mural, making a collage, singing a favourite song.
- For some children having a question box in the classroom may be very helpful and they can choose to submit their questions anonymously. Make a time when you will answer questions (read them beforehand) and if they want a private talk with a teacher they can also put a request in here but they must add their name!

### Frequently asked questions and sample answers

- Why did they die?
    - We don't know exactly why they died. It can make us worried and angry/cross when we don't know the answer to this. What we do know is that their body was very sick/not working properly/they were seriously hurt, and although the doctors tried hard to make them better it was not possible and their body stopped working and they died.
- Will it happen to me?
    - Usually when somebody is born they grow up and get to be quite old before they die. It is very unusual that a child dies. We don't expect you to die, we expect you will grow up and maybe even become a grandma/grandad – what will you look like when you are old do you think?
- Are they a ghost?
    - Ghosts are usually scary things, I don't think your friend would ever be anything scary. Some people believe that the part of us that makes us special can stay with us after a person has died, not in a scary way, but to help us remember that person and the love we had for them.
- Are their family okay?
    - It is so sad when somebody dies. They are probably feeling very sad, confused or angry right now, but there are lots of people looking after them and helping them. It is very kind of you to think of them, would you like to make something for them? (a picture, card, craft)
- What happens after you die?
    - Different faiths/cultures/people believe different things about what happens after death. Some people believe the special part of a person (that made them different and special) goes to a beautiful place, like heaven or to be among the stars. What do you believe?

The most important thing to remember when a child asks an unexpected question is that they deserve a good answer, not necessarily a fast answer. You might say that their question was very important, and you'd like to find some quiet time later in the day to answer this for them. You can say that you do not have an answer for them straight away but that you will come back to them with more information, once you have found it out. If their question is one that you cannot answer then we recommend you acknowledge how frustrating it is that there is not an answer to their question, but that they can always ask more questions and you will keep trying your best to answer them.

***Long-term considerations***

- Recognise that grief does not follow a set timeline. Continue offering support beyond the initial weeks, particularly around anniversaries, birthdays and significant school events.
- Monitor students who were close friends or siblings of the deceased child, speaking with their family often and offering additional emotional support as needed.
- Encourage open dialogue about grief in the school community to normalise conversations about loss.
- Be mindful of the impact on staff and provide ongoing mental health support, especially for those deeply affected by the child's death.
- Offer resources, such as books, counselling services and bereavement charities, for families who need further support. (Refer to Chapter 13 of this book for resources.)

## Conclusion

When there is a death in the school community the effects ripple outwards and affect individuals differently according to their relationship with the deceased and their own life experiences too. This chapter has provided practical examples of how we might have these difficult conversations. It is important that communication is clear, compassionate and timely and that all members of the community are considered. Remember that when a child asks an unexpected question, they deserve a good answer, not necessarily a fast answer.

Self-reflection questions to encourage deeper thinking:

- **Was there anything in these suggestions that surprised you?**
- **Why do you think that was?**
- **How would you use what you have learnt to approach the difficult task of informing children, parents, carers, guardians and staff of a death in the school community?**

## Bibliography

*NHS choices.* (no date). Available at: https://www.nhs.uk/conditions/end-of-life-care/where-you-can-have-care/hospice-care (Accessed: 3 January 2025).

# 10 Supporting minority groups

- What additional considerations of support may be needed for children from different minority groups, and what may interventions look like?

## Introduction

All of the chapters that have come before this one highlight how diverse and varied our experiences of grief and death are. Some children may wish to talk about their experiences openly with curiosity, whilst others may find conversations overwhelming and need time and space to process what has happened and how to discuss their emotions. These experiences can also be shaped by a child's background and home life, as we will explore in this tenth chapter.

The personal experiences of bereavement amongst minority children are greatly influenced by the context and culture within which the child lives (Cabrera and Stevenson, 2017).

'Complicated grief', as discussed in Chapter 4, may affect someone who has experienced the death of a loved one. Complicated grief is a condition where feelings of loss are so intense and long-lasting that they interfere with daily life and is also known as prolonged grief disorder, persistent complex bereavement disorder or traumatic grief. For children and young people from some backgrounds, there may be further differences in their experiences of death. For example, in a study by Douglas et al. (2021:1), 'black youth reported significantly elevated posttraumatic stress and maladaptive grief symptoms through higher polyvictimization and violent death exposure relative to white youth' and this may lead to more severe traumatic stress responses and complicated grief (Douglas et al., 2021). A more recent study by Tarazi (2024) into ethnoracially diverse young adults found their grief experiences were complex, 'underscoring the necessity of culturally sensitive interventions and support systems tailored to address their distinct experiences' (Tarazi, 2024).

So why may there be a difference in bereavement experiences in children from minority groups? Cabrera and Stevenson (2017) highlight three main factors that may lie behind these experiences of dying and loss: the child's worldview, communication and trust. Depending on the child's culture, or if they have religious beliefs, may also affect the grieving process and rituals that follow a death in the family. For example, 'many Hispanic communities commemorate the loss of their loved ones with promises or commitments. Open expressions of grief are acceptable. African American death rituals vary widely as a function of religious affiliation' (Cabrera and Stevenson, 2017). For this reason, it is essential that practitioners aim to build purposeful partnerships between school and home, to best understand the child's background and culture. Counsellors in particular should gather information about a child's cultural background when supporting them (Gonzalez and Bell, 2016).

## Supporting children and families from ethnic minority groups

Imagine trying to help someone who's sad when a loved one dies, but you don't know the best way. Mayland et al.'s review (2021) shows we need to learn more about how different groups of people handle grief. We need to find out how families and friends help and if the help we give is appropriate. Talking to people directly, and working together, will help us create better support for everyone. It's like building a special tool kit, made just for them. This next section helps you to consider some ways to support children and families from ethnic minority groups during the grieving process.

### *Cultural sensitivity*

Be aware of the cultural nuances of each group. Avoid making assumptions and be open to learning about their traditions and customs regarding death and grief (see also Chapter 6 on different views of death from the perspective of different religions and humanism).

### *Language accessibility*

Provide services and information in languages spoken by the community. Offer translation and interpretation services when needed, sending home letters and leaflets in different languages if helpful.

### *Inclusive practices*

Ensure that the services and resources available through the primary school are accessible and welcoming to people from diverse backgrounds.

### *Trauma-informed approach*

Recognise that some ethnic minority groups may have experienced historical trauma or ongoing discrimination, which can impact their grief process. Be mindful of this and offer trauma-informed support.

## Supporting children and families from Roma Communities or Traveller groups

Supporting children from Roma Communities or Traveller groups can also need consideration, especially in terms of supporting children who may not be in full attendance at school or may be moving locations. Some considerations for practitioners are listed below.

### Respect for traditions

Be respectful of their unique cultural practices and traditions related to death and mourning.

### Flexibility in support

Understand that their nomadic lifestyle may require flexible and adaptable support services.

### Community-based support

Consider if the school can arrange for providing support through community-based organisations or trusted individuals within the community.

### Language and cultural barriers

Be aware of language barriers and cultural differences that may hinder effective communication and support.

### Mental health considerations

Recognise that Roma Communities and Traveller groups may face additional mental health challenges due to discrimination and marginalisation. Consider if your school can signpost to culturally competent mental health support if desired by the families.

### Additional resources

- The Compassionate Friends: https://www.tcf.org.uk/r-useful-links/?cat=28
- Black, African and Asian Therapy Network (BAATN): https://www.baatn.org.uk/bamestream-bereavement-support-service/

Remember that providing effective support requires a deep understanding of the specific needs and cultural contexts of each group. Building trust and fostering open communication are essential for creating supportive environments for all individuals, regardless of their background or ethnicity.

## The Showmen community

Another minority group to be explored here is that of the travelling Showmen community.

Sheldon and Candace have also written a poem reflecting the unique lives of travellers and how a death in the community might impact a child; this is included in Chapter 13.

To end this chapter, we consider another minority group, that of prison-experienced families and the grief and loss of a parent going to jail. This guest contribution comes from Dr Stephen Scholes, Senior Lecturer specialising in Education at Queen Margaret University, Edinburgh, Scotland.

# Reframing childhood loss in Showmen Community - Candace G. Thomas, Co-Chair of ACERT. PhD Researcher at the University College Dublin

## Introduction

Showmen are a travelling community in the UK who have owned and operated fairgrounds for generations (Festing, 2013). As both a cultural minority and a business group, they are governed by the Showmen's Guild of Great Britain, which has around 4,000 members, 2,500 of whom are operating members with an estimated population of 25,000[1] (Greenfields et al., 2023). Showmen work in family-run firms, meaning generations live, work and raise children together. Children play active roles in the business and spend most of their time within the family unit. This makes the death of a loved one particularly poignant, when every caregiver in the extended family feels like a primary caregiver, due to the close-knit community we have illustrated below.

Showmen children may experience bereavement similarly to their peers; they often face added educational challenges linked to their identity and the effects of anti-gypsyism (Chadwick, 2024). They may also learn to navigate grief through traditional, community-led customs and practices that might seem unfamiliar or insignificant to educators (Whittle, 2023). Supporting a grieving Showmen child requires empathy and understanding of their unique cultural context.

Candace Thomas, a Showman woman from Scotland, is completing a PhD at University College Dublin. She is Co-Chair of ACERT and has led several charities focussed on education and well-being for her community. Sheldon Chadwick, a Showmen man from Lancashire, is pursuing a PhD at Liverpool John Moores University. He is the founder and CEO of the Showmen's Mental Health Awareness Charity and has worked on various education projects.

Both Candace and Sheldon experienced childhood grief within the Showmen community. Through a dual methodology of autoethnography, counter-storytelling and reflective poetry, rooted in Critical Race Theory, they seek to challenge dominant narratives about minoritised communities. Their aim is to foster meaningful dialogue about mental health in the Showmen community, highlighting its multigenerational, nuanced nature and deepening our understanding of childhood bereavement.

## Candace's story

Through the 1990s and 2000s my family and I travelled across Scotland, attending the same Fun Fairs, at the same time each year. This meant that we grew up with an extremely extended family, grandparents and great-grandparents, dozens of aunts and uncles, cousins and friends. The 'wagons' (mobile homes of various shapes and sizes) sat at the back of the 'Stuff' (fairground stalls and rides usually set in a circle with a row of centre positions) and a secure fence was erected around the entire perimeter of the Fair.[2] Our Dads would likely spend their days 'building up' the fair - painting, mending and laughing, and I am sure bickering over an extra couple of feet per position.

Our Mams would be back and forth between the stuff and the wagons taking on the responsibility of overseeing the smooth running of both. On a nice day everyone would have their windows and doors open for the fresh air. There were no concerns about anything going missing – the fair was our home, the people our family and everyone our caregivers.

We would run from home-to-home playing and laughing, if you needed to use the bathroom, get a drink or a plaster for a grazed knee, you went to the nearest wagon. When we were open, we would all play on the rides running from one to the next. The person 'minding' was a relative with a funny story or lesson on showmanship.

As you got into your early teenage years you would help out in running the Fairs. The extent to which you worked the Fair differed from family to family.[3] For some it was performing safe tasks, to the equivalent of a paper round, helping to build relationships with you and your family.

When someone dies in the Showmen community nothing stops. The show must go on. In memory of the deceased, you honour their hard work by matching it with your own. There is no crying and no pause. A funeral is arranged between the beginning of one fair and the start of the next. At the wake, people gather together, Showmen young and old to remark: 'He was a proper Showmen'. They sing, 'One more step along the world I go' a hymn fit for a Traveller.

Everyone attends the funeral in the morning and as a sign of respect goes back to work in the evening. Everything stays the same but there is one less open door to run to when you graze your knee. Everyone is sad with a smile. And no one talks about why.

### *Bibliography*

Chadwick, S. (2024). Its All a Show, (Public Exhibition) University of Sheffield, Liverpool John Moores University.

Festing, S. (2013). *Showmen: The Voice of Travelling Fair People*. Shaun Tyas, Spalding.

Greenfields, M., Chadwick, S., Coker, S. and Smith, D. (2023). *In-fair health*. Available at: https://www.aru.ac.uk/research/safe-and-inclusive-communities/in-fair-health.

Whittle, J. (2023). Ghosted Ground, (Public exhibition) University of Sheffield.

## Extending the idea of bereavement to prison-experienced families: Children's repeated encounters with grief and loss when a parent goes to jail – Dr Stephen C Scholes, Senior Lecturer in Education, Queen Margaret University, Edinburgh

### *Setting the scene*

Michael is a 31-year-old man working in construction, often working away and earning a good salary. He has a nine-year-old son, Logan. Logan lives with his mum, Louisa, through the week (about a thirty-minute drive away from Michael) and goes to the local primary school, where he gets on well with peers and is generally doing well. Logan goes to stay at his dad's every other weekend, and he enjoys doing this. Michael and Louisa get on okay, especially when it comes to ensuring Logan does well at school.Two and half years ago, Michael and two of his friends got into a fight with three other men on a night out. The police became involved, and in the end, they arrested Michael and his friends. They were detained but let back out and were to await a court case.

Michael and his two friends finally went to court two and a half years after the incident. Despite positive background reports about their excellent character and work ethic, the judge sentenced Michael to twenty months in prison. Michael went to court that day expecting community service, a fine, or some combination of non-custodial sentences on the advice of his lawyer. Regardless, he was sentenced and sent to prison immediately.

This section aims to encourage us to think more broadly about 'bereavement'. Here, we advocate understanding the experiences that children go through when someone in their family goes to prison as a form of 'bereavement'. Indeed, using Michael, Logan and Lousia's story, we go as far as to ask teachers and school communities to think about the nature of prison-experienced children's lives as (potentially) involving repeated encounters with a kind of loss and associated grief.

### The immediate aftermath

When a person goes to prison, their mobile phone and access to other means of communication are taken away. With the various processes and procedures in place, it can take a long time for individuals to communicate with their family, and there are limitations on who, how many people, and how long they can talk in the first instance. Michael's case was at 11am on the day he was sentenced, and he was in a cell at the nearest jail by 2pm on the day he was convicted. It was after 6pm before he could call his parents (who he called because he could remember their landline number) and let someone know what had happened.

Michael had to get the contact details of various people, including Logan's and Lousia's numbers, from his parents. Another followed the first call that evening about an hour later, which concerned itself with financial matters. Michael has a two-bed flat, where Logan has a room, and the monthly payments had to be sorted. Thankfully, Michael's family could handle these financial burdens, and Michael and Logan wouldn't have to lose their home.

Even before Logan knew anything about his dad's situation, the potential for loss of material aspects of their life together had presented itself. Unlike Michael's parents, many families cannot absorb the running costs of another house. So, as practitioners, we need to be alert to how a prison-experienced family might endure some or complete material loss. Thus, a custodial sentence could see a child removed from what they know, lose what they had and have to adjust to new material conditions, with the spectre of what they had before lingering in their thoughts.

As Logan stayed with his mum, Lousia, through the week, Michael's parents felt it was right to tell Lousia and that she should have a say in how Logan was informed. Lousia felt heartbroken for Michael. Following the phone call with his grandparents, Lousia told Logan what had happened. Logan was due to go to his dad's that weekend.

Logan has a calm disposition but can occasionally become a little bit boisterous. His time with his dad is a good re-set, and Logan enjoys time with him as they often get up to lots of different outdoor activities. Logan also likes to share things with his dad about his day and thoughts about life and ask the questions he doesn't want to ask his mum. And, almost every day, he gets to check in with his Dad via a text message exchange. The tricky thing for Lousia is that when she asked Logan how he felt about it all, Logan's responses were reserved and tended to be, 'Yeah, fine' or 'Yeah, I know I can talk, but I'm good'.

What Logan was not sharing with his mum in the hours and days after finding out his dad had been sent to prison was the difficult-to-articulate sense of loss that spans multiple aspects of his little life. Logan's routine had been lost, and his safety net of chats and check-ins with his dad was gone. Acknowledging that the loss is, in this case, temporary may help. Still, practitioners must recognise the potential for disorientation and distressed emotional responses to the new state of affairs that kids like Logan go through in such situations. They are left 'bereaved' when adults' decisions lead to prolonged absences.

### Continued encounters with loss

Arranging a visit to someone in prison isn't easy. Various arrangements must be made within a multifaceted system that can be subject to change at short notice. Logan visited his dad about two weeks after the court case but had managed to speak with him on the phone at least twice a week in the interim. With his grandparents accompanying him, Logan was okay about going to visit. They had a good forty minutes together. Michael spent time explaining to Logan what had happened and made a promise that once he was out, this would never happen again. Logan. There was no clear plan for a future visit, but Logan was not sure he wanted to visit again; the end of the visit was upsetting when he had to say goodbye to his dad. A month into his incarceration, it remains unclear exactly when Michael might get out. Somewhat frustratingly for the family, there were discussions around early release, and while Logan knows this, he's been told that it's still unclear.

In this final excerpt, there are two points of consideration when the focus is on seeing experiences of imprisonment as bereavement. First, visitations are a site where, although there may be celebration and joy at the prospect of reconnecting, the reality of the loss becomes all too real when they end. Children are reminded of their new normal and the loss of what was. Second, the uncertainty of what comes after the initial loss and the repeated reminder of the loss at the end of each visit, much like when someone dies, raises its head when future visits are not immediately known. All the more so when the possibility of early release remains fuzzy, too. Children's loved ones and the kids themselves stay in perpetual limbo, offering the conditions wherein grief can resurface as reminders of the loss arise throughout a sentence.

### Thinking more about prison-experienced families, children and bereavement

This section has outlined some critical points using a short story to scaffold the exploration. This story is only one of many others that can involve longer custodial sentences, more traumatic circumstances and more complicated family dynamics. For example, another story could be told of a child with additional support for learning needs whose verbal communication and comprehension of abstract notions demand repeated reminders of the loss of a parent's presence. This complexity is something we need to keep in mind when we learn of children in our classroom experiencing a member of their family going to prison. Especially when, unlike in Logan's case, we often do not have anything like the details we need to understand the true extent of their loss.

### Further reading

- Kincaid, S., Roberts, M. and Kane, E. (2019). *Children of prisoners: Fixing a broken system.* Available at: https://www.crestadvisory.com/post/children-of-prisoners-fixing-a-broken-system.
- Baldwin, L. and Epstein, R. (2017). *Short but not sweet: A study of the impact of short custodial sentences on mothers and their children.* Available at: https://dora.dmu.ac.uk/server/api/core/bitstreams/0c3b89ec-6974-4af0-92c7-b6070a34d8b5/content.
- Barkas, B., Deacon, K., Foster, R., Jardine, C., Primrose, K. and Troy, V. (2021). *Getting it right for families affected by imprisonment: Lessons from ten years of research.* Available at: https://pure.strath.ac.uk/ws/portalfiles/portal/124842198/Barkas_etal_SCCJR_2021_Getting_it_right_for_families_affected_by_imprisonment.pdf

## Conclusion

Everyone's experience of grief is unique, but when practitioners are supporting children and families from minority groups and backgrounds there may be additional conditions that can be considered to make the support as helpful and relevant as it can be.

- What are some of the whole school approaches that can be employed to support families?
- What is the value of a trauma-informed approach?
- Reflect on Logan's case study in the contribution in this chapter; if Logan was in your class at school, what ongoing support would you offer to him?

## Notes

1. There are conflicting statistics as to the number of people in the Showmen's Guild of Great Britain Scottish section https://scottishshowmensguild.org/. Thse Scottish Sections website suggests there are 400 members (family firms) and 2,000 community members. Fair Scotland a local charity suggests that this number is double or triple https://fairglasgow.wordpress.com/. The 2021 census was the first time in which Showmen were counted but a reliable count is yet to introduced https://www.scotlandscensus.gov.uk/2022-results/scotlands-census-2022-rounded-population-estimates/#:~:text=%22Scotland's%20population%20grew%20to%205.4,ever%20recorded%20by%20Scotland's%20Census.%22.
2. A position is a plot of land designated each year to the same person. Showmen become members of the Showmen's Guild of Great Britain https://showmensguild.co.uk/ to ensure their rights are maintained at each Fair.
3. The majority of Showmen (male and female) would have worked in the Fair from 11/12 years old. They would operate a ride or stall when open. We would often take breaks or stand talking with friends close by. Other tasks would be helping to build up and pull down, maintain the rides and clean, cook and look after the wagons.

## Bibliography

Cabrera, F. and Stevenson, R. (Eds.). (2017). Dealing with Loss and Grief of Minority Children in an Urban Setting. In *Children, Adolescents, and Death* (pp. 203-217). Routledge.

Douglas, R.D., Alvis, L.M., Rooney, E.E., Busby, D.R. and Kaplow, J.B. (2021). Racial, ethnic, and neighborhood income disparities in childhood posttraumatic stress and grief: Exploring indirect effects through trauma exposure and bereavement. *Journal of Traumatic Stress*, 34(5), 929-942.

Gonzalez, C.L. and Bell, H. (2016). Child-centered play therapy for Hispanic children with traumatic grief: Cultural implications for treatment outcomes. *International Journal of Play Therapy*, 25(3), 146.

Mayland, C.R., Powell, R.A., Clarke, G.C., Ebenso, B. and Allsop, M.J. (2021). Bereavement care for ethnic minority communities: A systematic review of access to, models of, outcomes from, and satisfaction with, service provision. *PLoS One*, 16(6), e0252188.

Tarazi, R.R. (2024). *The Shadow of Grief: Understanding Grief among Ethnoracially Diverse Young Adults*. Cuny Academic Works.

# 11 Lived experiences of grief and bereavement

- What are your own personal experiences of grief?
- Have you supported children in class who have been bereaved?
- Do you feel that you were well supported to meet the child's needs?

## Introduction

This chapter explores lived experiences of grief and bereavement from adults who have been bereaved as children and those who have supported children in grief. They share reflections on how they themselves were supported and how bereavement support could be improved.

### Marie

Marie Greenhalgh's (co-author of this book) Mother died when she was just 7. Feelings she has experienced on her grief journey so far include loss, fear, worry, anger, injustice, heartache, sadness, anxiety, depression, longing and determination.

> My mum died when I was seven, so thirty-six years ago. There was very little support in school, I mostly remember that my sister (aged five) was allowed to bring in her teddy, and I had a photo of my mum in my school bag. But really, that was the extent of the support, although there may have been more that I was not aware of. I mostly remember feeling like everyone (staff and pupils) were always looking at us but not really knowing what to say.
>
> The biggest thing I would have found helpful is having a trusted adult to speak to, and people who verbalised being there for me and understanding. Even when we moved schools, and later when I went on to secondary school it was never spoken about or acknowledged. I also worried so much about my sister and my dad, especially when I was separated from them by being in school, so a way to check in with them when I needed to would have helped. There was a lack of awareness of language used, I remember letters being handed out and the teacher telling the class 'take this home to your mum' and I just sat there thinking 'but I don't have a mum anymore'.

> **Other things that Marie identified would have helped:**
> - Access to school counsellors or psychologists who are trained to help children process grief and loss.
> - Opportunities to connect with peers who have gone through similar experiences, perhaps through support groups or special programs.
> - Designated areas where I could have gone if I needed a break or some quiet time.
> - Information on external resources, such as bereavement groups or community support groups, that can offer additional help.

## Joanne Mullan, Psychology Course Lead at The University of Glasgow

Joanne Mullan's Nan died when she was in primary school. Here she offers a personal reflection and identifies the key elements from her teacher, Mrs Marshall's actions which made a real difference. Her poem inspired by these experiences is included in our resources chapter.

> My nan was my kinship carer and my absolute world. She picked me up from school every day, celebrated every small achievement and knew how to make ordinary days feel special (I still love Twister ice lollies!). But everything changed when she died. I have this very vivid memory of sitting in class, the sun shining in the windows brightly with the clock ticking towards three feeling excited about her waiting for me at the school gate. And then reality crashed over me; I remembered that she was gone, and she wouldn't ever pick me up again. The weight of that loss was overwhelming and all-consuming, and despite usually being such an attentive child, I zoned out and completed missed what was going on in the classroom and why the other children were celebrating. It was likely to have been something our wonderful teacher, Mrs Marshall, had organised for us.
>
> When Mrs Marshall noticed that I was crying, she came straight over. I can still feel her gentle touch moving my hair behind my ear, allowing me to cry, showing she understood why without me having to say a word. And giving me the coveted purple bunny stamp to take home because she knew I would be upset about my smudged spelling test. I didn't have to say anything, she knew me well enough. By whispering eight small words in my ear "You are going to make her so proud", she instilled a determination that has lived on inside me my whole life. Even now, every decision I make, I ask myself "Would nan be proud of this?".
>
> That kindness and those eight small words whispered in a bereaved child's ear, have fuelled an adventurous, happy, well-travelled life; a successful career; a loving family of my own and shaped a granddaughter that my nan would indeed be proud of.

### How to be more Mrs Marshall - Joanne Mullan

*Stay observant*

Grief can manifest in different ways – sudden outbursts, inability to focus and withdrawal. Being attentive to these changes can help you to provide the best support when it's needed.

*Crying is ok*

Adults are often so quick to rush in to stop children crying when what they need is a good release of whatever emotion is consuming them, and this is very important for grief. Mrs Marshall allowed that to happen, for as long as I needed.

*It's the little things (Isn't it always?)*

Simple acts, like Mrs Marshall giving me the bunny stamp because she knew I loved it, mean so much to children. Find out the little things that bring them joy and use them to help them to feel seen and cared for.

*The power of words*

Encouraging words can instil hope and help to motivate children to keep moving forward. It is important to not only acknowledge the sadness but also let the child know that they have purpose in the world and still have much to achieve and that you believe in them.

Supporting a bereaved child doesn't require big gestures, it's the littlest things that often make the biggest difference. By embodying the compassion and understanding that Mrs. Marshall showed me, educators can make a profound impact on a child's healing journey. Being more like Mrs Marshall means noticing the needs of your students, providing a safe and supportive environment and sprinkling kindness and encouragement into every interaction.

## Emma Marfleet, founder of The Marfleet Foundation

Emma Marfleet is an educator who reflects on her own experiences of supporting bereaved children in her early days of being in the classroom and how her personal encounter with grief and the experience of her children has shaped her desire to help others in this field.

### Lessons learned for supporting bereaved children in schools

Out of all the goals in life to aspire to, knowing how to support grieving children in schools isn't likely to be at the top of anyone's list. It wasn't on mine when I began training to become a primary school teacher in the mid-90s. But life has a way of leading us down unexpected paths, and for me, it's where my professional and personal journeys have converged.

I taught in a variety of primary schools, developing my teaching style and learning from the children in my care. I led in different curriculum areas before becoming a Deputy Headteacher, a role in which I felt settled and then ready to start my own family. It was during this time, before I had children of my own, that I taught a nine-year-old named Aaron.

Aaron was in my first class at a new school where I was a class-based Deputy Headteacher. Aaron's dad had died two years earlier, his mum had a new partner and Aaron had a new baby brother. I assumed that he had 'moved on' from his grief, had adjusted to his new life and was content with the stability it offered. At that time, I had not experienced the death of someone close to me, so I had no point of reference other than to treat and to teach Aaron as I would do any other child in my class. What I didn't understand then was that grief isn't something you simply 'move on' from. I took two active steps to support Aaron in school. First, I used the term 'grown-ups' instead of 'mums and dads' to avoid alienating him. Second, I made sure to prepare him in advance for a lesson or task that might trigger difficult emotions. While these steps were well-intentioned, I now realise that there was so much more I could have done. I understand better now what it truly means to be a bereaved child in a mainstream school environment, as I see my own children cope with their grief following the death of their dad in June 2019 when they were only eight, six and three years old.

Daniel, at eight-years-old, wanted to go back to school two days after his dad died. Matthew, at six years, wanted to follow his big brother's lead. Six years later, they both remember how returning to school gave them a sense of comfort, routine and connection with their friends. Daniel's class sent home a card with messages from his classmates, telling him they were thinking of him and looking forward to his return. His response surprised me, as he shrugged and put it on the pile of comics by his bed. He didn't want the attention; he wanted his 'normal' back. But as an adult, I knew that his normal would look different from now on.

Supporting my children's return to school started with good communication. I saw school staff at drop-offs and pick-ups and was given time to chat if needed. Matthew's Year 1 teacher supported his class by sharing bereavement books (mostly about pets) before he returned to school. She explained that Matthew's dad had died, that he might be sad and that their job was to help him. A teaching assistant with whom Matthew had a good relationship was timetabled to stay in his class, providing him with someone he could turn to.

Matthew remembers helping with out-of-class jobs and sometimes choosing whether to sit with his class or work in a small group with the teaching assistant. 'Matthew was very open, willing and brave to talk about his dad's death', they told me.

> Whenever he did, we stopped everything to have an impromptu talk about how he was feeling or to address any questions. There was never a 'bad' time to talk about

it. We wanted Matthew and everyone else to know that if they need to talk or ask questions, they could.

It felt like a culture of care was wrapped around my six-year-old when he needed it most.

Good communication was also key in Daniel's return to school in Year 4. I created a family mantra, 'Be brave, Be kind', as our symbolic armour. Grief often kicks when people don't say the right things, even with the best intentions. His teacher adopted it as the class motto, and I loved seeing it displayed as a large graffiti sign in his classroom.

As my boys grow older, I see firsthand how their grief doesn't follow any clear timeline. It resurfaces at anniversaries, milestones, and in unexpected moments. Reflecting on Aaron's journey, I see the same was true for him. Two years on, my role as his class teacher was just as crucial as it had been for the teacher who first helped him reintegrate into school and routine during those early days of his bereavement.

I see this clearly too in my youngest son, Sam, who was just a toddler when his dad died, too young to grasp the full impact, yet deeply affected by his absence. He carried the weight of loss, surrounded by the confusing emotions of grief at the time. As he grows older, his understanding deepens, bringing up new feelings, questions and behaviours. To help him make sense of it all, I work closely with his school, meeting his new teacher at the start of each academic year to discuss his experience and current emotional needs. Together, we focus on both proactive and reactive support, equipping him with tools that will benefit him for life.

These experiences led me to create The Marfleet Foundation, a space where schools can access resources, training and real-life experiences to better support grieving children. My goal is to empower educators with the knowledge and confidence to make a difference, so no child faces grief alone or unsupported. Grief is a shared human experience, and the more we talk about it openly, the better equipped we are to guide children toward a future where grief is understood and where the needs of grievers are better considered. It has allowed me to channel my energy into something positive amidst the pain following my husband's death, while also being present for my own children as they navigate their grief in their own way and at their own pace.

As a teacher, I know that schools work hard to create nurturing environments, but without the proper training and understanding of child bereavement, educators may miss crucial opportunities to help grieving children feel seen and supported. Good support requires a holistic approach: one that combines proactive planning, reactive care and an ongoing commitment to meeting children where they are in their grief. Proactive planning involves identifying where death and grief appear in the curriculum and tailoring the approach to acknowledge and reassure the child's experience, rather than alienating them. Reactive care means being ready to respond to a child's emotional needs as they arise, prioritising their emotional well-being.

Looking back, I know I supported Aaron with care and empathy, but I wish I had taken the time to simply sit next to him and listen to how he felt in school, in my classroom. If I had, I would have known his triggers, rather than relying on my assumptions, and I could have given him time to talk about his dad. My children's primary school have taken this concept further, creating a group where bereaved children can talk about their loved one, process their grief and share coping strategies. This approach empowers them to adapt to the changes in their lives while feeling understood and supported.

Daniel and Matthew are now in secondary school, navigating school life with increasing independence. They've carried the tools they learned during primary school with them, continuing to build fulfilling lives and emotional resilience as they grow. This is an ongoing journey, but their experiences reaffirm the long-term value of grief-aware education. It's not just about helping bereaved children cope, but it's about helping them thrive.

## Conclusion

You have the power to change a child's experience of bereavement so that unlike Marie where staff didn't know what to say so they said little or nothing, as Anna Lise says in the foreword 'Just say something'. Also take inspiration from Joanne's teacher, Mrs Marshall, it is the small things that make a big difference. Compassion and empathy go a long way when you are feeling sad and vulnerable in grief, as is clear communication and an understanding that grief doesn't have a timeline. A child's awareness of their bereavement will change over time as they grow and develop and so the support they need may alter too. Much can be learned from listening to those who have experienced bereavement which enables you to support them in the most appropriate way. An understanding and listening ear are appreciated.

Self-reflection questions to encourage deeper thinking:

- **How do you feel your own personal experiences of grief impact on how you support others?**
- **After reading this chapter, how will you change your approach (if at all) to supporting children in class who have been bereaved?**
- **What additional support do you need to meet a grieving child's needs?**

# 12 How to support and look after yourself

## Introduction

Teaching is tough. Juggling lesson plans, marking, managing classroom dynamics, pressure for results, Ofsted, all while managing your own work life balance and well-being. It's no surprise that many teachers feel overwhelmed. In fact, nearly half say their workload is too much to handle most of the time. Now, add supporting a bereaved child to that. It's emotional and challenging and can take a toll on you. You're not just teaching anymore; you're helping a child navigate one of life's toughest experiences. Supporting a grieving child is important, but it's not easy. You'll feel a range of emotions, from sadness and compassion to frustration and helplessness, made even more challenging if there is a death within the school itself such as that of a child or staff member. And constant exposure to the pain of others can leave you feeling drained and overwhelmed. In this chapter, we'll explore why your well-being matters when supporting bereaved children. We'll look at the impact it can have on you, both emotionally and psychologically. And most importantly, we'll talk about self-care strategies to help you navigate this challenging but important aspect of teaching.

## Your welfare: why it is important

Teaching is already an incredibly challenging role, and teacher well-being is a much talked about topic. A survey by the National Education Union (NEU) in 2023 found around half of teachers (48%) said that their workload is unmanageable, either most of the time or all of the time. Stress levels are high, with more than a third of teachers saying they are stressed 80% or more of the time ((National Education Union, 2023). According to the Health and Safety Executive (HSE), teaching professionals have one of the highest rates of work-related stress, depression or anxiety in the UK (www.hse.gov.uk, no date). The Education Support Partnership reported that nearly three-quarters of teachers experienced some form of mental health issue, such as stress or anxiety, in the past year (Education Support, 2023).

Child Bereavement UK's 2019 research revealed:

- 86% of respondents said they'd experienced a death in the school community.
- Only 34% felt their school was equipped to manage a death when it occurred in their school community.

- Only 2% said death and bereavement was a practical focus of the curriculum at their school.
- 92% said schools should prepare ahead in case they experienced a bereavement.
- Only 10% of teachers had received training during Initial Teacher Training or subsequent professional development.
- 89% had experienced no bereavement training.

## Supporting a child in your classroom

Supporting a child who has been bereaved can be a deeply emotional and impactful experience for educators. It's not just about providing academic guidance; it's about being there for a child who is navigating one of life's most profound and challenging experiences, the loss of a loved one.

Imagine a child in your classroom, once full of laughter and enthusiasm, suddenly carrying the weight of grief on their small shoulders. You see the sparkle fade from their eyes, replaced by a profound sadness that seems to seep into every corner of their being. As a teacher, you can't help but feel this in your heart, knowing that you're witnessing a child grapple with emotions far beyond their years.

Supporting a bereaved child means more than just offering words of comfort; it means being a pillar of strength when their world feels like it's crumbling around them. It means creating a safe space where they can express their feelings openly, without fear of judgement or misunderstanding. It means listening with empathy, holding their hand through the storm of emotions and letting them know that they're not alone.

But supporting a grieving child can take its toll. It's a delicate balancing act between offering support and managing your own emotions. Supporting a bereaved child can have profound effects on educators, both emotionally and psychologically. Here are some of the ways it can impact you:

Supporting a bereaved child often involves deeply empathising with their pain and grief. As you witness their struggle, you may find yourself experiencing a range of emotions, from sadness and compassion to frustration or helplessness. Your heart may ache for the child, and their grief may resonate deeply within you.

Constant exposure to the pain and suffering of others, particularly children, can lead to vicarious trauma or secondary traumatic stress. As you support a bereaved child through their journey of grief, you may find yourself absorbing some of their trauma, which can manifest as symptoms similar to those experienced by the child, such as intrusive thoughts, nightmares or emotional numbness.

Supporting a bereaved child may also trigger your own unresolved grief or past traumas. The child's experiences may awaken memories or emotions related to losses in your own life, making it challenging to remain objective and composed in your role as a supportive figure.

It's natural to form strong bonds with the pupils you support, especially in moments of vulnerability such as grief. However, this closeness can sometimes blur professional boundaries, leading to feelings of over-identification or an inability to maintain appropriate distance, which may impact your ability to provide effective support.

Supporting a bereaved child can be emotionally draining, leaving you feeling depleted and overwhelmed. It may be challenging to prioritise your own self-care needs when you're focussed on meeting the needs of others, leading to burnout, compassion fatigue or diminished job satisfaction over time.

Despite the challenges, supporting a bereaved child can also bring a sense of fulfilment and purpose to your work as an educator. Witnessing the child's resilience, growth and healing can be deeply rewarding and reaffirm your commitment to making a positive difference in the lives of your students.

Supporting a bereaved child can enhance your skills as an educator, teaching you valuable lessons about empathy, resilience and the importance of fostering a supportive and inclusive learning environment. It may also inspire you to seek out additional training or resources to better support grieving students in the future.

## Impact of teacher bereavement on supporting bereaved pupils

Teachers who have experienced bereavement themselves face unique challenges when a child in their class undergoes a similar experience. I was bereaved as a child, and again as a young adult at the start of my career, and I know firsthand that this does impact how you feel. Having gone through personal loss can significantly impact how you provide support, presenting both challenges and opportunities for empathy and connection.

Personal bereavement can enhance a teacher's empathy towards a grieving student. Teachers who have navigated their own grief may find it easier to relate to and understand the emotional turmoil faced by the child. This heightened empathy can foster a stronger bond and provide the child with a sense of being truly understood.

However, a teacher's own grief can also act as an emotional trigger when supporting a bereaved child. If you're a teacher who has experienced bereavement, being exposed to a student's grief can have significant emotional impacts. Constant exposure to another's grief, especially when it mirrors your own experiences, can intensify feelings of helplessness and sadness. This phenomenon is known as secondary trauma, which can lead to secondary traumatic stress. Symptoms include flashbacks, avoidance of certain scenarios, negative changes in beliefs and hyperarousal. Over time, this can result in compassion fatigue and burnout, reducing your ability to provide support and leading to feelings of numbness and detachment (www.educationsupport.org.uk, no date a).

Balancing personal emotions while maintaining professional boundaries is crucial. Teachers might struggle with over-identification with the bereaved child, making it challenging to provide objective support. This emotional involvement can lead to burnout and compassion fatigue, affecting overall job satisfaction and effectiveness as an educator (Education Support, 2023).

To mitigate these challenges, it is essential for teachers to seek support from colleagues, supervisors or mental health professionals. Engaging in peer support networks or supervision sessions can provide a space to discuss and process their experiences, gaining valuable insights and validation. Additionally, professional development opportunities focussed on bereavement support can enhance a teacher's confidence and skills in managing these complex situations.

## Self-care strategies when supporting a bereaved child

Taking care of yourself while supporting a bereaved child is crucial for maintaining your own well-being and effectiveness as an educator. Here are some strategies for self-care during this challenging time:

Establish clear boundaries between your professional responsibilities and personal life. Allocate specific times for supporting the bereaved child and ensure that you also have time for your own needs and activities outside of work.

Don't hesitate to reach out to colleagues, friends or mental health professionals for support. Share your experiences and feelings with trusted individuals who can offer empathy, validation and practical advice. In Chapter 13 we list a number of organisations such as 'Child Bereavement UK' with their web addresses and some also have helpline numbers which we have included for your use. Also the website www.showmensmentalhealth.com includes many links to great mental health resources which may be helpful to you and the young people you teach.

Be kind to yourself and recognise that it's normal to feel a range of emotions when supporting a bereaved child. Give yourself permission to experience and express your feelings without judgement.

Dedicate time to activities that nourish your mind, body and spirit. This could include exercise, hobbies, meditation, spending time with loved ones or simply engaging in activities that bring you joy and relaxation.

Understand that you can't fix or alleviate the child's grief entirely. Set realistic expectations for yourself and acknowledge that supporting a bereaved child is a process that requires patience, empathy and time.

Cultivate mindfulness through practices such as deep breathing, meditation or mindfulness exercises. Mindfulness can help you stay grounded in the present moment, manage stress and cultivate resilience.

Allow yourself to take breaks throughout the day to recharge and rejuvenate. Even short breaks can help you decompress and maintain perspective during emotionally challenging situations.

Prioritise your physical health by eating nutritious meals, getting enough sleep and staying hydrated. Neglecting basic needs can exacerbate stress and emotional exhaustion.

Seek out professional development opportunities related to supporting grieving students. Enhancing your knowledge and skills in this area can boost your confidence and effectiveness as a supportive educator.

Cultivate gratitude by focussing on the positive aspects of your work and life. Reflect on moments of connection, growth and resilience, and express gratitude for the opportunity to make a difference in the lives of your students.

Recognising and being aware of your own triggers and past experiences is crucial when supporting a bereaved child. Here's how you can navigate this aspect of self-awareness:

Take time to reflect on your own experiences with grief and loss. Identify any situations, memories or emotions that may serve as triggers for you. These triggers could be related to past losses in your own life or other sensitive experiences.

*How to support and look after yourself*  85

- Pay attention to your emotional responses when interacting with the bereaved child. Notice if certain topics or behaviours evoke strong reactions in you, such as sadness, anxiety or frustration. These reactions may indicate areas where you have personal triggers.
- Be compassionate and gentle with yourself as you explore your triggers and past experiences. Acknowledge that it's natural to have emotional responses and remind yourself that you're doing the best you can in a challenging situation.
- Develop coping strategies to manage your triggers and emotional responses effectively. This could involve techniques such as deep breathing, grounding exercises or mindfulness practices to help you stay present and regulated during difficult moments.
- Recognise when certain situations or conversations are triggering for you and establish appropriate boundaries to protect your emotional well-being. It's okay to take a step back or seek support from colleagues or supervisors when needed.
- If you find that your triggers or past experiences significantly impact your ability to support the bereaved child, consider seeking professional support from a therapist or counsellor. A mental health professional can help you explore and process your emotions in a safe and supportive environment.
- Utilise supervision sessions or peer support networks within your school or organisation to discuss and process your experiences. Sharing your challenges and seeking feedback from colleagues can provide valuable insights and validation.

Engaging in personal therapy or counselling can be beneficial for educators, especially when navigating complex emotional issues such as supporting bereaved children. Therapy can provide a confidential space to explore your triggers and past experiences in-depth.

## Conclusion

Remember that prioritising self-care is not selfish; it's essential for maintaining your own well-being and capacity to support others effectively. By taking care of yourself, you'll be better equipped to navigate the challenges of supporting a bereaved child with compassion, resilience and empathy.

Self-reflection questions to encourage deeper thinking:

- **How does the emotional toll of supporting a bereaved child impact my overall well-being, and what strategies can I use to maintain balance in my professional and personal life?**
- **What barriers might prevent me from feeling fully prepared to support a grieving student, and how can I overcome them through training or self-reflection?**
- **In what ways can I create a supportive classroom environment while also ensuring I have the necessary support to manage my own emotional resilience?**

## Resources

Child Bereavement UK: Offers training for professionals and resources for supporting grieving children. Available at: https://www.childbereavementuk.org/.

Education Support: Support for teachers, including free and confidential helpline 08000 562 561. Available at: https://www.educationsupport.org.uk/.

Grief Encounter: Another organisation offering resources and support for dealing with child bereavement. Available at: https://www.griefencounter.org.uk/.

Winston's Wish: Provides support for bereaved children, including guidance for teachers. Available at: https://www.winstonswish.org/.

## Bibliography

Adams, K., Erle, S., Ungerer, S. and Sossi, M. (2024). Supporting primary teachers to address loss and death in the classroom: A case study of an interdisciplinary, creative pedagogical intervention using education, children's literature, architecture/design and the arts. *Pastoral Care in Education*, *43*(2), 1-24. https://doi.org/10.1080/02643944.2024.2327447.

Child Bereavement UK. (2019). *Child Bereavement UK*. [online] Available at: https://www.childbereavementuk.org/.

Education Support. (2023). *Teacher Wellbeing Index 2023*. [online] Available at: https://www.education-support.org.uk/resources/for-organisations/research/teacher-wellbeing-index/.

National Education Union. (2023). *State of education 2023: Workload and wellbeing*. [online] Available at: https://neu.org.uk/latest/press-releases/state-education-2023-workload-and-wellbeing.

www.educationsupport.org.uk. (no date, a). *The effects of secondary traumatic stress on teachers and education*. [online] Available at: https://www.educationsupport.org.uk/resources/for-individuals/videos/secondary-trauma/.

www.educationsupport.org.uk. (no date, b). *Work-related stress in the teaching profession has increased for a third consecutive year*. [online] Available at: https://www.educationsupport.org.uk/news-and-events/news/work-related-stress-in-the-teaching-profession-has-increased-for-a-third-consecutive-year/.

www.hse.gov.uk. (no date). *Stress at work - Resources and useful links*. [online] Available at: https://www.hse.gov.uk/stress/resources.htm.

www.showmensmentalhealth.com. (no date). *Mental health resources*. [online] Available at: https://www.showmensmentalhealth.com/mental-health-resources/.

# 13 Resource bank

- How might you help children to learn about death, loss and bereavement?
- What types of activities might help children who have been recently bereaved?
- What other books might you read for further information as a school adult wanting to support children who are grieving?

## Introduction

The purpose of this chapter is a reference bank including activities, picture books, further reading and organisations you may find helpful. We would advocate a cross-curricular approach; by that we are not suggesting for one minute a topic on 'Death, dying and bereavement' it is a very sensitive topic, and whilst it should not be shied away from, it must be approached gently and with compassion. What we mean by cross-curricular in this sense is a thread running through the curriculum, carefully chosen texts in English lessons, such as some of those we include in this chapter. In science, exploring the life cycles of animals and plants acknowledging that death is part of this cycle, RE lessons may explore the religious rituals around death and in PSHE discussing the emotions associated with grief and providing pupils the tools to discuss death and grief, to support themselves, friends and family. Some refer to this as 'death literacy' in the same way we use the term 'emotional literacy'. These are just a few suggestions but are by no means exhaustive. This approach will help to normalise death as a part of life in a gentle way though it may offer opportunities for those who sadly have been bereaved whether this is recent or historic, to explore their emotions and to feel supported and less alone. As the caring adult in the classroom, make sure you are aware of those for whom the topic may be particularly challenging and need extra support.

Some of the books we suggest may be helpful in the immediate aftermath of a death, quite separate to a planned curriculum thread. You may also wish to include some of the resources that we highlight to the appendix of your bereavement policy.

## Activities to support children navigating bereavement

### Dilma De Araujo, lecturer and researcher, SEND consultant

Dilma De Araujo is an experienced lecturer, researcher and SEND specialist with over a decade in education across public and private sectors. She has worked with students from early years to higher education, focussing on special educational needs and education policy and promoting gender inclusion and diversity. Currently, she works in the Higher Education field. Dilma mentors adults with special needs and has spearheaded humanitarian projects supporting SEND schools in Africa and Asia. She holds a master's in inclusive education policies and pursuing a Doctorate in Educational Studies. Dilma is passionate about fostering innovation and leadership to drive inclusion in education. She has kindly contributed this section on 'activities'.

### *Children and bereavement support: How can playing activities support children's development during grief and loss?*

Play is an essential activity for children's learning, physical, emotional and cognitive development. After an experience of grief and loss, playing activities can be crucial for helping children cope with complex emotional events. Children might act out a death situation or include ideas about death in their routine play activities as a process of emotional healing. As a special educational needs' teacher, it is crucial to provide support to learners with mental health, learning, physical or sensory needs (such as Profound and Multiple Learning Difficulties (PMLD), Autistic Spectrum Disorder (ASD) and Severe Learning Disabilities (SLD)). These professionals have substantial knowledge concerning coping with emotional and psychological experiences in challenging times. Hence, some approaches and activities may support educational staff, such as primary school teachers, teaching assistants and school leaders, in supporting children's development during grief and loss.

Thus, UC Davis Children's Hospital's (no date) studies highlight practical and artistic ways to support children's emotional and cognitive progress. Playing activities can boost skills and abilities by using creative learning strategies to facilitate communication and fostering connections. Similarly, physical movements and direct contact with natural resources and environments benefit children's ability to genuinely express their emotions, concerns and ideas.

### *Self-expression and awareness via drawing, writing and painting activities*

Writing or drawing **Gratitude Hearts for family or friends**. In these communication messages, it is vital to support children in expressing how individuals have encouraged and inspired them constructively. Aiming to support children in building healthy relationships, coping interaction skills and resilience and releasing emotions using storytelling, arts and crafts.

Supporting children in embracing their sense of identity and belonging, aiming to assess and understand their feelings and ideas about tools they can use to manage them. For example, establishing an empathic dialogue with children, then providing them with **Small Paper Notes** with sticking emojis associated with their mood, emotional and mental state.

Based on the previous activities, teachers can use **Empathic Conversations**, to create a reflection pathway with students (by drawing circles or chains). Aiming to support children in expressing their feelings and finding constructive ways to generate self-awareness, motivation and critical thinking ideas.

Encouraging children to elaborate a **Memory Jar or Journaling** where they express their feelings and ideas by writing and drawings. These feelings and ideas can be discussed with educational mentors, coaches and family members. Some of the sentences or drawings could start with the following eliciting statements:

Now, I want... I need... I hope...
Feelings of grief, loss, sadness,
I can change things by...
After the death, school/friendship/family has been...
If I feel lonely, I will...

By making sense of life experiences, children can be encouraged to play and develop learning skills close to natural resources. They can create a **Family Stone Garden** using paint or markers to write characteristics about their loved ones or draw the best family memories on the stones. Then, the stones can be placed in a unique place in their home, garden or bedroom. A family memories photo album or scrapbook can also include pictures, messages, wishes and important citations.

### Self-resilience and confidence via music and dance therapy activities

Encouraging physical movements and sensory engagement, children can create a **Song Playlist** based on family and friends' memories, and the children can sing and dance together.

**Emotions Freezing Dance Movements** – Children's body movements while dancing to the sound of the music support their sense of balance (vestibular system) and sense of space (proprioception system). These movements are one way to express feelings related to grief. Expressing emotions through movements might be mixing or copying familiar sounds and rhythms. **Joining different dancing styles and facial expressions** while performing big or small movements. **Jumping, swaying or singing** along are mechanisms of communication, interaction and emotional self-regulation approaches. **Dancing** can be performed standing, seated or even lying down, making it accessible and inclusive. Thus, educators can select a song. While the music is playing, they can call out a feeling or perform a facial expression related to the selected song and encourage children to dance and move in ways that reflect their mood or emotional state.

Using music as a creative self-expression approach, play children's favourite music and support them in creating a **Remembrance Sunflower.** The centre can include the name and/or picture or place of the family member/friend. Write something special about the person or a unique memory in each flower petal.

**Performing Yoga Movements/Sessions**, applying restorative body poses to address emotional states. Movements such as child's pose, bug pose, twist pose, gorilla pose, cross-legs pose, seated forward fold and bridge poses.

## Self-regulating and emotional balancing approaches before the introduction of activities

Establish grounding roles and clarify expectations before the implementation of any activity:

Children should take ten slow breaths. Pinwheels, bubbles and/or balloons can be used to develop blowing practice movements. Deep breathing can also be beneficial for children's emotional decompression.

Introductory activities should be related to the main topic the session with a song, dance movements, drawing or painting activity providing real scenarios in the classroom or family context. Engaging the different human senses and call attention to the following:

**5 things children might see**
**4 things children can hear**
**3 things children could touch**
**2 things children like to smell**
**1 thing children would like to taste**

Mirroring activity ensures that children focus on the main activity. Educators take turns with children pretending they are mimes and following each other's actions. To start with, they may wave their bodies or hands back and forth, bring a finger to their nose or touch their hands to their toes. Using a finger labyrinth can represent a simple way to call attention to the present situation or activity.

## Conclusion

Playing activities related to self-expression and awareness, as well as self-resilience and confidence approaches, are crucial to children's holistic learning perspectives and expectations. Teachers and educators may notice that the children often recall events related to grief and loss or ask questions. To support children in making sense of these complex situations, it is vital to encourage them to explore and share their feelings and emotions. Hence, drawing, painting, music, dancing and outdoor activities can empower mental and perceptual contexts that often influence emotional, expressive, developmental and social abilities.

## Emma Marfleet, founder of The Marfleet Foundation

Emma has a degree in Education from Homerton College, Cambridge University. She has worked as a class teacher in KS1 and KS2, offered outreach support in a range of primary schools as an Advanced Skills Teacher, and she has an experience of school leadership. She is a widowed mother to three school-aged boys. She has kindly contributed this section on creating safe spaces for grieving children which includes activity plans to accompany four core picture books on the topic of death and grief. There is something comforting about the nature of a picture book when dealing with the topics of death, dying and bereavement. Many of these books can be read aloud to the class for sensitive discussion but they can also be used in a therapeutic way in small groups as illustrated by Emma's tailored activity plans.

## Creating safe spaces for grieving children

The National Institute for Clinical Excellence (NICE, 2004) and Childhood Bereavement Network (2017) highlight that bereaved children need a supportive response from their existing networks to thrive. Child Bereavement UK (no date) adds that schools can support grieving pupils by continuing their usual activities while remaining mindful of the bereavement. It's my experience that educators who want to support grieving children must show this awareness and provide both proactive planning and reactive care, always putting the child's emotional needs first. Many children, however, will benefit from dedicated time and care taken out of their school routine to further nurture their emotional needs due to their experience of bereavement at a young age. With this in mind, I have developed guided activity plans to provide ongoing support for bereaved children in school, going beyond proactive planning and reactive care, to offer more for the supportive response that bereaved children need to thrive.

These guided activities use high-quality picture books which address themes of love, loss, death and grieving as inspiration for both conversation and craft. I provide guidance on how to use each book with bereaved children, including key questions to ask, support notes and ways to close each session, ensuring children feel supported, reassured and comfortable enough to return to their school day. Depending on this book, these activities delve deeper into themes such as memories, connections and attachment, feelings, coping strategies and change.

Best practice involves creating a safe and supportive space for discussing death and grief - ideally a calm, uninterrupted environment outside the usual classroom setting. A Nurture Room or Reflective Space works well, as it provides an established, calm and safe area within a busy school. Arrange the seating to best suit the activity, and don't hesitate to adjust it with the children for different parts of the session; physical movement often helps focus and concentrate and can ease tension after discussing challenging emotions or experiences (think about how children often 'puddle jump' in and out of dealing with big emotions). The session should be led by a trusted adult with a positive and established relationship with the children. Each session should encourage compassionate language, offer non-judgemental support and allow children to express their thoughts and feelings freely, without fear of judgement. Consider setting these ground rules and expectations at the beginning of each session, ensuring children know they can contribute as much or as little as they feel comfortable.

Supporting a bereaved child though can be challenging. It's important for an educator's own mental health and professional development to take time to reflect after each session. Reflecting on questions such as: What worked well, and why? What questions or discussions surprised me? What will I do differently next time? - either on your own or in a conversation with a colleague - can help guide your approach moving forward.

92  *Supporting bereaved children in the primary classroom*

**Badger's Parting Gifts - Susan Varley**

This long-lasting book on love and loss is endorsed by Child Bereavement UK and includes advice on how to share it with children. The story explores the role an older loved one has in our lives and the things they help us know how to do. These skills become their 'parting gift' to us after they have died. With a focus on how old Badger is when he dies, I recommend this book to use with children when a grandparent has died.

**Recommended age range for this activity session: Key stage 1 and lower key stage 2**

**Themes:**                          **Memories**                          **Connections**

*Image 13.1* Image of a child making a 'parting gifts jar' as described in the activity. Image provided by Richard Cranefield Photography

*Activity 13.1 - Suggested activities for Badger's Parting Gifts*

**The Marfleet Foundation**
Supporting Bereaved Children In Schools

Activity Sheet #15
*'Badger's Parting Gifts'*
By Susan Varley

## INTRODUCTION

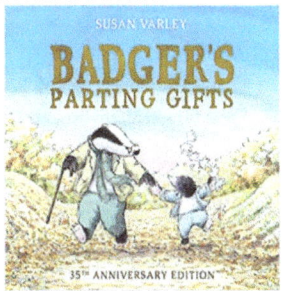

Look at the cover of this book with the children and search for clues that hint at what the story might be about. Most children will notice that Badger looks old (with a walking stick and glasses), and the word "parting" in the title may suggest that he's facing the end of his life. Make sure the children feel comfortable exploring this book with you, and let them know that today's session will create a safe space for open conversations and for sharing feelings about love, loss, and grief.

## KEY QUESTIONS

Can you list the special memories the friends share about Badger?

Can you think of something your loved one taught you how to do?

The author tells us that Badger gave each of his friends a 'parting gift to treasure always.' What do you think of this idea?

Can you think of something your loved one taught you how to do?

**Support Note:**
On the first page of this book, we learn that Badger is 'very old' and that he knows 'he must soon die'. It's important to make sure the children in the group who have experienced the loss of a loved one feel comfortable discussing the death of someone who is elderly and who had time to prepare their loved ones. Children whose parent or sibling died at a young age may want to talk about how, sometimes, death doesn't follow the natural order of things.

You may also want to consider the phrase 'parting gift'. Badger taught his friends skills – things he could do before they could – and these teachings became his 'gift' to them. This is a gift in the sense of passing on knowledge or skills, much like what a parent/carer, grandparent, or an older sibling might do. The 'parting gift' is the gift of what has been learned, and it may not necessarily be something given because the person knew they would soon die.

Be mindful that children bereaved at a young age might not have had the opportunity to learn something directly from their loved one or may not remember it. If appropriate, the 'gifts' they might share could include physical traits such as the same colour hair or eyes as their loved one, or a shared love for a hobby like reading, drawing, or sports.

Copyright © 2024 - The Marfleet Foundation - All Rights Reserved           www.themarfleetfoundation.org

## Activity – Making A Parting Gifts Box or Jar

**Each Child Will Need:**
- [ ] An empty box or jar (a clean jam jar works well)
- [ ] Several small pieces of paper
- [ ] Pens
- [ ] A variety of craft supplies to personalise each box or jar

**Instructions:**
1. Give each child a piece of paper to write or draw something their loved one taught them how to do. They can then fold it carefully and place it into their box or jar.
2. Repeat this activity as many times as each child wishes, adding new 'parting gifts' with each round. Some children may want to expand on these memories, recalling the first time they learned how to do something with their loved one. Other children may need prompts to help them remember what they did together. Encourage them to think about skills they can do now, at their current age, that they once had to learn when they were younger.
3. Finally, spend time decorating the boxes or jars and talking about the special memories each child holds of their loved ones, and the special parting gifts they have received.

## Closing the Session

Recap the story by reminding the children that Badger gave each of his friends a different parting gift, each one special to the individual. Ask the children if any of them have made paper chains like Badger taught Mole, or if they can ice skate like Badger taught Frog? Who taught them these things? How about knotting a tie like Badger taught Fox? Have any of them baked gingerbread like Badger taught Mrs Rabbit?

Then, remind the children of the sentence on the last page of the book: "Whenever Badger's name was mentioned, someone remembered another story that made them all smile." Reassure the children that even when we grieve the death of someone special and feel sad about them no longer being with us, we can still talk about the special memories and the things that we did with them when they were alive. These memories are parting gifts, and they are ours to keep and cherish.

If appropriate, invite the children to share some of their own parting gifts from their special boxes or jars. Encourage them to share their work with their family at home.

---

**Teacher Reflection**

Supporting a bereaved child can be hard. It is important for you own mental health and for your ongoing development as an educational practitioner to take time to reflect on the session you've just delivered.
On your own, or in conversation with a colleague, consider the following questions:
What worked well and why? What questions or discussion was I surprised by? What will I do differently next time?

---

For more resources like this one please visit www.themarfleetfoundation.org

## *The Invisible String* - Patrice Karst

This is a wonderful book to use with children, as it celebrates the ongoing connection we have with the people we care about, even when they're not physically with us. This book includes the idea of a connection that continues after someone has died, making it an important resource for bereaved children. I enjoyed sharing this book with my children because it helped us talk not only about our 'invisible string' to their daddy but also about the important people who continue to support us. We also loved finding the hidden hearts in each illustration, which made the experience feel truly interactive.

### *Recommended age range for this activity session: All primary school ages*

**Themes:** **Feelings** **Connection and Attachment**

*Image 13.2* Image of a heart and string poster as described in the activity. Image provided by Richard Cranefield Photography

## Activity 13.2 - Suggested activities for The Invisible String

Activity Sheet #1
*'The Invisible String'*
By Patrick Karst

### INTRODUCTION

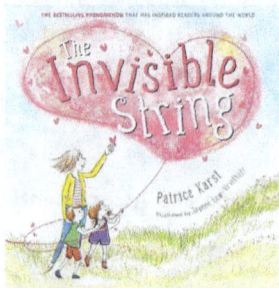

Create a safe and supportive environment for talking about death and grief by reminding the children that all emotions are welcome in this space, and that it's equally ok to share or not share our feelings. Reassure them that our group work encourages open conversations, where everyone's voice will be heard.

Before reading this book with a bereaved child, tell them that it is about being connected to people we love with an invisible string. Tell them that it includes one of the children asking, "Can my string reach all the way to Uncle Brian in heaven?"

When the children are ready, read the book together taking time to find the hearts hidden in each illustration.

### KEY QUESTIONS

Who can you think of now at the end of one of your invisible strings?

How does thinking about them make you feel?

Can you think of something you have done with them which made you happy?

**Support Note:**

Bereaved children may talk about their special person who has died, or someone who is still alive. Both are ok! It helps to hear who is special to them and you can learn about their support network if they choose someone who is still alive.

Copyright © 2024 - The Marfleet Foundation - All Rights Reserved

www.themarfleetfoundation.org

## Activity – Making A Heart And String Poster

**Each Child Will Need:**
- [ ] A4 or A3 Paper for the poster
- [ ] Other paper for cutting out
- [ ] String or wool
- [ ] Coloured pens and/or pencils
- [ ] Scissors
- [ ] Glue

**Instructions:**
1. Cut out hearts to represent yourself and at least one other special person. Name them and stick them onto your poster.
2. Using glue and wool or string, create a visible connection between two of the hearts. Encourage creativity to make the wool or string as looped, curled and as visually and interestingly tangled as you can.
3. Using coloured pens and/or pencils, note things along the wool/string that you have done with that person, e.g. play board games, football, tv time. Encourage a bereaved child to talk about happy memories of spending time with their special person whilst working on the activity.
4. Repeat the above, linking each of the hearts to each other if your poster has included more than two hearts.

## Closing the Session

The Invisible String is a book of love. *"Even though you can't see it, you can feel it deep in your heart and know that you are always connected to the ones you love."* In this session, we have made a visible reminder of some of the special things that connect us to our special people. Even though we can't always see them, we are connected and it's a thread that never need break.

Tell each child what you like about their posters using the sentence starters, *"I can see that you…"* and, *"I like that you have…"*

---

Teacher Reflection

Supporting a bereaved child can be hard. It is important for you own mental health and for your ongoing development as an educational practitioner to take time to reflect on the session you've just delivered.
On your own, or in conversation with a colleague, consider the following questions:
What worked well and why? What questions or discussion was I surprised by? What will I do differently next time?

---

For more resources like this one please visit www.themarfleetfoundation.org

Copyright © 2024 - The Marfleet Foundation - All Rights Reserved    www.themarfleetfoundation.org

98  *Supporting bereaved children in the primary classroom*

### *When They Died* – Poppy Gibson

This book is sensitively written and encourages reflection on death and grief through a clear format of questions and answers. While not every question has an answer, it provides a supportive way to respond to the many questions children (and adults!) often have after the death of a loved one. Reading this book with my children revealed questions about their daddy's death that they wanted to ask but were afraid to in case they upset me. Some of the questions gave me the opportunity to share reasons for things that happened, which they were either too young to know about or didn't remember from that time.

***Recommended age range for this activity session: Key stage 2***

**Themes:**                                **Feelings**                                **Coping Strategies**

*Image 13.3* Children making a group 'griefiti wall' as described in the activity. Image provided by Richard Cranefield Photography

*Activity 13.3 Suggested activities for When they Died*

Activity Sheet #17
*'When They Died'*
By Poppy Gibson

## INTRODUCTION

This book thoughtfully addresses conversations about death and grief for children, presenting them openly through questions and answers. Before starting the session, ensure that the children feel safe and comfortable discussing their feelings.
Remind them that it's ok to experience different emotions and reassure them that they can share as much or as little as they like— no feeling is wrong. Encourage respect for one another's thoughts and let them know that all feelings are valid in this space.

## DISCUSSION GUIDE

This session starts with a guided discussion around the book's blurb and cover illustration (in that order), followed by a group activity and sharing the book together.

**1. Introduce the topic:**
Begin the session by inviting the children to share their thoughts on why some people find it difficult to talk about death. Let them know that today's session will focus on exploring questions surrounding death and how we think about it.

**2. Introduce the book:**
Introduce the book When They Died by reading the blurb on the back. Ask them to share their ideas on what the 'mysterious protagonist' might look like. Once you've discussed their ideas, reveal the cover and ask how they feel about the illustrator's interpretation of the 'mysterious protagonist.' Does it match or differ from their expectations? What do they think the illustrator is trying to convey through this image?

**3. Exploring the book's content:**
Now that we've explored the blurb and the illustration, what do we expect from the book? Agree with the likely response that this book will focus on questions and answers surrounding death. Explain that some questions will be easier to answer, some may be more challenging, and some may not have an answer at all.

*Support Note:*
Following the structure of group discussion, activity, and then reading the book together allows you to learn how the children feel talking about death and which questions are most concerning them at the outset. It also offers insight into the language they use when discussing grief.

Before continuing with Part 2, remind them again that this is a safe space for sharing thoughts and feelings.

Asking them to share their ideas about what the 'mysterious protagonist' looks like will reveal their personal interpretations of what 'tall size and spooky' means. This also prepares them for the cover of the book which features a cemetery.

## Activity – Griefiti Wall

**You Will Need:**
- [ ] A large sheet of paper
      For a wall-like effect, lightly sketch brick patterns on the paper
- [ ] Coloured markers or felt-tip pens

**Instructions:**
Place the paper on the floor, attach it to a wall, or position it on a table that the children can easily move around. Explain that together, you'll create a graffiti wall with questions about death before reading today's book.
Ask the children to write any questions they have about death on the wall using the bright-coloured pens. Encourage them to write in a graffiti style, using a variety of colours, and to move around the paper as they write.
For extra support, display question words like "why," "what," "when," "where," and "will" to help prompt ideas
Some children may also want to explore their own artistic interpretation of the mysterious protagonist, which could be another interesting avenue to explore inspired by the book.

## Reading and Closing the Session

After creating the graffiti wall together, ask the children to sit comfortably and read the book. Pause when a question from the wall appears in the story, and discuss their thoughts on the mysterious protagonist's answers. Once you've finished the book, refer back to the graffiti wall and check if there are any questions that weren't addressed in the book. Can we come up with an answer together?
Finally, remind the children that they can talk to a trusted adult at home or at school if today's session has brought up any new questions or feelings about death or their own experiences with bereavement. Reassure them that, as we talked about at the start of the session, many people find it difficult to talk about death. They've done really well today in sharing their thoughts and feelings, and that's something to be proud of.

---

**Teacher Reflection**

Supporting a bereaved child can be hard. It is important for you own mental health and for your ongoing development as an educational practitioner to take time to reflect on the session you've just delivered.
On your own, or in conversation with a colleague, consider the following questions:
What worked well and why? What questions or discussion was I surprised by? What will I do differently next time?

---

For more resources like this one please visit www.themarfleetfoundation.org

## Michael Rosen's *Sad Book* - Michael Rosen

Michael Rosen pours his personal experience of grief into this brilliant book and creates a gift for all children, not just those who are bereaved. But it's not a comfortable read and children will need supporting if they choose to look at it. Bereaved children though will take encouragement from how Michael expresses his feelings and how he swings between extreme feelings of sadness and loss to the hilarity of how ridiculous and silly grief can make us behave when we feel so completely overwhelmed by it. My own children laughed out loud when I shared this book with them, and it was both the comfort and relief we needed at such an impossibly sad time after their daddy died.

**Recommended age range for this activity session: Upper key stage 2**

**Themes:**         **Feelings**          **Coping Strategies**          **Memories**

*Image 13.4* Image of a decorated picture frame as described in the activity. Image provided by Richard Cranefield Photography

## Activity 13.4 - Suggested activities for Michael Rosen's Sad Book

Activity Sheet #8
*'Michael Rosen's Sad Book'*
By Michael Rosen

### INTRODUCTION

Start the session by asking the children what they already know about Michael Rosen and his poetry. They may know that he nearly died of Covid-19 and wrote about his experience. They may know that his son Eddie died. Explain that this book is about Michael's experience of the grief he felt after Eddie's death.

Prepare the children for the possibility that they may find similarities in Michael's experience and their own. Read this book together pausing to allow space for discussion as you go. Be sure to explain that even though this book is about grief, it might also make us laugh!

### KEY QUESTIONS

What does grief feel like?

What other emotions can it make you feel?

What can you do when you feel sad?

How does that help you?

**Support Note:**
Start with a discussion **about** the book answering questions as Michael would.
Then discuss the children's personal answers to the questions, learning **from** the book.

By openly sharing his personal story, Michael speaks to grievers of all ages and covers many topics which can be explored in a safe and supportive environment with bereaved children in school.
These include:
- how feeling sad can look and how we can sometimes hide our feelings so not to upset others
- the emotions which can come with grief, e.g. anger
- that sadness and grief can affect anyone, at any time
- how grief makes changes to your life
- coping strategies including talking to others, doing 'crazy' things, things that make you happy, writing
- how our memories make us feel
- Michael also touches on thoughts of suicide, "I just want to disappear." Consider what support you might need if this topic is likely to arise during your discussion. It might be helpful to ask another adult from school to join your group, or to seek advice from childhood bereavement charities for guidance on how to navigate this sensitive topic with children.

## Activity – Decorating A Picture Frame

Turn to Quentin Blake's final illustration in the book and ask the children what they think is in the picture frame Michael is looking at. It's likely to be a photo of a happy memory of Eddie. Tell the children that they are going to decorate their own picture frame which they can take home to put a special photo in for themselves.

**Each Child Will Need:**

- [ ] A blank photo frame from a craft shop or cut strong cardboard
- [ ] Paints, felt-tip pens, crayons...
- [ ] Optional extra decorating art supplies e.g. sequins, pompoms, glitter, stickers etc.

**Instructions:**

Decorate the frames with words, phrases and/or pictures of things that remind you of your special person who has died. Encourage the sharing of happy memories and explore how it feels to talk about them.

If your group needs more direction, ask them first select a paint colour that reminds them of their loved one and to paint their frame all over in this base colour. Ask them how the colour makes them feel and which memories they are thinking of. When the base layer of paint is dry, ask the children to add drawings of what their loved one liked or any hobbies they had, e.g. yoga, cats, motorcycles, books, footballs etc. Pens will give more detail to the drawings than paint.

Some children may want to write a poem instead of putting a photograph into the frame. Michael's poem may inspire them to write about their feelings but they can equally write about a happy memory of being with their loved one. They might want to follow a structure similar to Michael's but thinking about their happy memory. Look for patterns and repetitions used by Michael to inspire their own creative writing.

## Closing the Session

Ask each child if they would like to share their photo frame with the group and possibly the happy memories they were thinking about whilst they were decorating it. They may have a photo in mind to put into the frame and would like to share that with the group. Hopefully, they feel good thinking about happy memories of their loved one during this session. Even though the person we love has died, we can still enjoy talking about them and sharing our memories of them with others.

Michael used his gift for writing to think about (process) his strong feelings of grief after Eddie died. Have the children done anything similar? Perhaps they've written in a journal or drawn in a sketchbook. It's never too late to start and using a creative process is an incredibly powerful and successful way for people of all ages to process their grief. This discussion may encourage a bereaved child in your group to have a go, let them know that you are there if they would like to share their work with you or to discuss the idea further.

---

**Teacher Reflection**

Supporting a bereaved child can be hard. It is important for your own mental health and for your ongoing development as an educational practitioner to take time to reflect on the session you've just delivered.
On your own, or in conversation with a colleague, consider the following questions:
What worked well and why? What questions or discussion was I surprised by? What will I do differently next time?

---

For more resources like this one please visit www.themarfleetfoundation.org

## Joanne Mullan, Psychology Course Lead at The University of Glasgow

Joanne is an enthusiastic and dedicated education professional based in Scotland. She has a multidisciplinary background with degrees in Education, Psychology and a Diploma in Counselling and Cognitive Behaviour Therapy, and she is currently studying for a Doctorate in Educational Leadership. She champions mental health and is the founder of 'Starra Education' a training service in the field of mental health in education.

This beautiful poem has been written especially for this book as a personal reflection of Joanne's childhood bereavement. This could be used as an explorative text as well as inspiration for the children's own expressions of grief, either through personal experience or after contemplating grief and how it can feel.

### You Are Going To Make Her So Proud
#### Joanne Mullan

I look at the big clock, it's ten to three! And it's sunny!

Sunny Friday means when nan picks me up, she'll take me to the park and get me a Twister ice lolly on the way!

She's going to be so happy about my spelling test as well, I can't wait to tell her!

And then I remember.

The rest of the class are cheering, I don't know why, I wasn't listening. The bell is ringing, and they are all rushing out to go and play in the sun.

My spelling test is ruined. My tears have smudged the purple stamp, my favourite one, with the little bunny.

Mrs Marshall comes over beside me. She tucks my hair behind my ear and holds my hand.

"I know you miss her. You let those tears out."

Eventually, I stop crying. Mrs Marshall wipes my face gently and takes me over to her desk. She gets the purple bunny stamp, puts it in my bag, and gives me a wink.

She takes me out to the gate and, as she gives me cuddle, she whispers in my ear,

"You are going to make her so proud".

And from then on, I made sure that I did.

Sheldon W Chadwick is Chief Executive of The Showmen's Mental Health Awareness Charity and researcher at Liverpool John Moores University, Candace G Thomas is Co-Chair of ACERT and Ph.D. Researcher at the University College Dublin. Both Candace and Sheldon experienced childhood grief within the Showmen community and have captured the essence of what it was like to be a bereaved child within the Showmen community. It is particularly poignant that they state the bereavement happened whilst away from school as this may apply to many children from the travelling community or not. This poem could be used to explore unique challenges of particular communities as well as to inspire children to write their own poems on experiences of bereavement.

**No Matter Where you are, Education Comes First**
**Sheldon W Chadwick - Chief Executive of The Showmen's Mental Health Awareness Charity. Researcher at Liverpool John Moores University**

(To be performed for my teacher)
Learning on the move
Education packs
Books on the trail
From place to place
Stained with Toffee apple dye
Infused with the smell of onions

My homework was different
It had its own life
Seen its own sights
Taught by strangers who became friends
Marked by traveller teachers
Crumpled in the corners
But still all there

It's a myth that we don't care
We may be Showmen
But we are also...
Mothers and fathers
Brothers and sisters
Doctors and lawyers
Engineers and rocket scientists.

So miss, please remember this
As I come back in the winter
I have caught up
I won't hinder your Ofsted inspection
I wasn't neglected
I am here and ready to learn

Although while I was travelling
I did lose a family member
And it hurts
We still moved the fair
We stuck together
But seeing her ride
Blue and yellow are their colours
Lorrie's with her name on top
The position her Wagon stood,
It is empty on the yard

And I have to tell you
She will no longer be dropping me off
Or picking me up

I know it was when I was away
But now I am here
Is it normal to feel this way
Can they ever come back?

Miss, can I ask you a question?
Will this pain ever stop?
Because my love hasn't

like candy floss
Her words are stuck in my head

"No matter where you are, education comes first"
Please help me not fail

## Publications for further reading – Anna Lise Gordon, Professor of Education, St Mary's University

These publications have been curated by Professor Anna Lise Gordon from the School of Education at St Mary's University, London. The School of Education at St Mary's is at the forefront of efforts to increase teachers' awareness of, and confidence in, supporting children and young people who experience bereavement.

A 'starter for ten' list of useful reports and research articles for further reading which are freely available online and accessible to busy teachers:

- Bereavement is everyone's business (November 2022). UK Commission on Bereavement Report. Available at: https://bereavementcommission.org.uk/ukcb-findings/

- 'I don't understand why you are upset': public and parental views on grief education and support for bereaved children in UK schools – Marie Curie report (2024). Available at: https://www.mariecurie.org.uk/globalassets/media/documents/policy/policy-publications/2024/grief-education_uknations_charts_v5_22.02.24_final.pdf
- Compassionate School Communities – Embedding a culture and practice of grief education and bereavement support in educational settings, Marie Curie Northern Ireland Report. Available at: https://www.mariecurie.org.uk/document/compassionate-school-communities-in-northern-ireland
- Improving bereavement support in schools. Child Bereavement UK report (2018). Available at: https://www.childbereavementuk.org/Handlers/Download.ashx?IDMF=fa7a443b-636d-4238-af12-accedec84419" no longer seems to be current. Please provide an updated link
- Consequences of childhood bereavement in the context of the British school system – Winston's Wish report (2019). Available at: https://winstonswish.org/wp-content/uploads/2019/06/COCB.pdf
- 'The one thing guaranteed in life and yet they won't teach you about it': The case for mandatory grief education in UK schools – Dawson, L., Hare, R., Selman, L., Boseley, T. and Penny, A. Available at: https://www.bereavementjournal.org/index.php/bcj/article/view/1082/1121
- Grief Matters – Exploring the impact of bereavement and grief on learning for all – Gordon, A.L. (2022). *British Educational Research Association (BERA)*. Available at: https://www.bera.ac.uk/publication/grief-matters
- Bereavement in Education Summit Report (2024). Gordon, A.L. Available at: https://www.stmarys.ac.uk/research/docs/bereavement-in-education-report.pdf
- Bereavement in the primary school: a critical consideration of the nature, incidence, impact and possible responses – Porter, J. (2016). Available at: https://insight.cumbria.ac.uk/id/eprint/2864/1/Porter_BereavementInThePrimarySchool.pdf
- Addressing the bereavement needs of children in school: an evaluation of bereavement training for school communities – McManus, E. and Paul, S. Available at: https://pure.strath.ac.uk/ws/portalfiles/portal/86781100/McManus_Paul_IS_2019_Addressing_the_bereavement_needs_of_children_in_school.pdf

## Organisations

We cannot endorse all services listed; this is merely a signpost to assist those wanting to explore support options for others or themselves. We have included websites to serve as databases for international and national bereavement organisations, national organisations in the UK (many similar models will operate globally) and a few local organisations to illustrate the type of support you may wish to search for in your locality.

Many childhood bereavement organisations include useful documents in different ways that adults can best support children; a number of sites also include PSHE lesson plans such as Winston's Wish. Many like Child Bereavement UK have a list of children's books on loss, death and grief, and some like the Marfleet foundation also include activities related to a number of books beyond those included in this chapter.

Online databases for bereavement support:

https://www.ataloss.org has over 2,000 local and national (UK) bereavement services listed 'helping bereaved people find support and well-being'. Look under the 'Find Support' tab where you can filter by location and age of person needing support as well as other specific parameters. In the USA a similar site is https://evermore.org/grief-support-directory and of course searches for 'Childhood bereavement support in my area' will provide suggestions for readers around the globe.

## National organisations

### Childhood Bereavement Network

https://childhoodbereavementnetwork.org.uk

'The hub for those supporting bereaved children and young people across the UK'.

CBN advocates for bereaved children, young people and those supporting them, influences policy and public understanding, supports professionals with knowledge and resources they need to deliver high-quality, accessible bereavement care, signposts to sources of bereavement support and generates new ideas and approaches to improving bereavement care for children.

### Child Bereavement UK

https://www.childbereavementuk.org

'Child Bereavement UK helps families to rebuild their lives when a child grieves or when a child dies'.

Child Bereavement UK offers bereavement support for families, training for professionals as well as publications and resources.

0800 02 888 40 or helpline@childbereavementuk.org

### Cruse Bereavement Support

https://www.cruse.org.uk

'Grief can be overwhelming, you don't have to deal with it alone'.

Cruse is a recognised bereavement charity for adults but specific advice on childhood bereavement can be found under the tabs: understanding grief > grief experiences> children, young people and grief.

It provides some answers to the following questions: Should children come to funerals? What do children understand about death? What are the signs of grief in a child?

0808 808 1677

## Grief Encounter

https://www.griefencounter.org.uk
   'A world where no child is left to grieve alone'.
   To help bereaved children, young people and their families to find hope and healing. Grief Encounter works closely with individuals, families, schools and professionals and their offering includes counselling, workshops, online resources and training.
   0808 802 0111 (Weekdays 9:30 am–3 pm)

## Scotty's Little Soldiers

https://www.scottyslittlesoldiers.co.uk
   Helps ensure long-term support for bereaved military children.
   Scotty's Little Soldiers aims to provide relief from the effects of grief for bereaved military children and young people who have experienced the death of a parent who served in the British Forces.

## The Marfleet Foundation

https://www.themarfleetfoundation.org
   'Empowering teachers to support grieving children in schools'.
   The Marfleet Foundation provides advice, training and resources that reassure and empower schools to be prepared when there is a bereavement within their community.

## Winston's Wish

https://winstonswish.org
   'Giving hope to grieving children'.
   Winston's Wish charity supports bereaved children, young people, their families and the professionals who support them.
   08088 020 21 or email: ask@winstonswish.org

# Local Organisations

These local organisations are provided as examples; an online search may prove fruitful for similar services in your area.

## Families in Grief

https://familiesingrief.org
   'To help all bereaved families living in North Devon and the Torridge area feel better and less alone in their grief'.
   Families in Grief (FIG) offers bereavement support for families, children and professionals in North Devon and the Torridge area.

### Pete's Dragons

https://www.petesdragons.org.uk

'To reach those impacted by suicide and provide support that is timely, appropriate and carried out by professionals'.

Offering support in North Devon and Somerset for children and young people, professionals and schools.

### SeeSaw

https://seesaw.org.uk

'Grief support for children and young people in Oxfordshire'.

SeeSaw provides support to families (where there are children in the immediate family up to the age of 18) who live in Oxfordshire. They offer a 'pre-bereavement' service if the person with a terminal diagnosis is being treated at Oxfordshire hospitals or in the care of an Oxfordshire hospice. They offer direct support to children aged from 5 to 18 if a parent/carer or sibling is dying or has died. They offer FREE online training for those working with bereaved children and young people in Oxfordshire.

## Conclusion

This chapter is just a starting point, suggestions for activities the whole class can get involved in and some for small groups or individuals. We have included a handful of links to further reading and handpicked four children's books to help you with resources we have used ourselves, though there are many more children's books available for you to explore and some of the organisations we have signposted you to will have more extensive lists on their websites.

Self-reflection questions to encourage deeper thinking:

- **Do you feel more confident to address bereavement and grief with these activities at your fingertips? If not, where will you look next to build your knowledge and confidence?**
- **Which activities do you think are more suitable for children who have been recently bereaved and for those who have been bereaved a while?**
- **What other resources might you explore for further information as a school adult wanting to3 support children who are grieving?**

## Bibliography

### Books

Gibson, P., and Russo, A. (2024). *When They Died*. Crow Tales Publishing.
Karst, P. (2012). *Invisible String*. Scholastic.
Rosen, M. (2011). *Michael Rosen's Sad Book*. Walker Books.
Varley, S. (1987). *Badger's Parting Gifts*. Andersen Press.

## Journals and reports

Child Bereavement UK. (no date). *Primary schools*. [online] Available at: https://www.childbereavementuk.org/primary-schools.

Child Mind Institute. (2024). *Helping children deal with grief*. Available at: https://childmind.org/article/helping-children-deal-grief/ (Accessed: 28 December 2024).

Childhood Bereavement Network. (2017). *Grief matters for children*. [online] Available at: https://childhoodbereavementnetwork.org.uk/sites/default/files/uploads/attachments/grief-matters-for-children-2017.pdf (Accessed: 28 December 2024).

Children Bereavement Centre. (no date). *Play therapy*. Available at: https://www.childrensbereavementcentre.co.uk/play-therapy (Accessed: 28 December 2024).

East Renfrewshire Educational Psychology Service. (2021). *Supporting children affected by bereavement, loss and grief*. Available at: https://blogs.glowscotland.org.uk/er/PsychologicalService/school-staff/support-with-bereavement-and-loss (Accessed: 28 December 2024).

Glasgow Educational Psychology Service. (no date). *Loss and bereavement*. Available at: https://blogs.glowscotland.org.uk/glowblogs/glasgowpsychologicalservice/loss-bereavement/ (Accessed: 28 December 2024).

National Institute for Clinical Excellence. (2004). *Improving supportive and palliative care for adults with cancer*. [online], pp.160-161. Available at: https://www.nice.org.uk/guidance/csg4/resources/improving-supportive-and-palliative-care-for-adults-with-cancer-pdf-773375005.

UC Davis Children's Hospital. (no date). *Activities for grieving children and families*. Child Life and Creative Arts Therapy. Available at: https://health.ucdavis.edu/children/patient-education/bereavement-activities (Accessed: 28 December 2024).

# 14 Conclusion

- After reading this book, do you feel better prepared to support the young people in your classroom?
- Are you aware of resources and organisations to support you?
- Do you know if your school has a user-friendly bereavement policy or how to write/update one?

It has been an absolute privilege to write this book to assist classroom practitioners and wider school staff to support children who have been bereaved. We are delighted to have worked with some incredible collaborators along the way and hope that we have been able to reduce the fear of needing specialist training, 'saying the wrong thing' and have given you the courage to 'just say something'. Of course, specialist bereavement training is a bonus, and many of the charities we have mentioned offer this, but each and everyone of us has the ability to support children who are struggling academically or who need additional emotional support so we can also walk alongside those children who are grieving with confidence and compassion.

In this book we have highlighted some of the challenges faced in primary schools when dealing with the topics of death, dying, grief and bereavement and offered insights and guidance to break down these barriers. Hopefully you now understand the difference between loss, grief and bereavement and how each of these affects our experience and perspective on the world.

We presented four theories around phases of grief, noting that these models are frameworks to help us understand the grieving process and not rigid rules. Grief is a highly individual experience, and people may move through different stages at their own pace and in their own way. Case studies have been included from those with educational and palliative care backgrounds, many also with lived experiences of childhood bereavement. The purpose of this is to present different viewpoints and personal experiences to illustrate the needs of those who are bereaved and to shine a floodlight (a broad range of views) on a topic so rarely discussed in society, let alone in school.

The varying ways children may comprehend and react to death have been outlined, highlighting the importance of tailored support strategies for each age group and children who may require distinct approaches to understand and process loss. Faith may also impact a child's understanding of death, and we provide a very brief overview for the busy educator of how the major world religions or those with a humanist perspective view death, as well as some of the rituals surrounding it that the children in your class may experience. Additionally, we have addressed the broader impact of bereavement on the entire class and enhance the emotional well-being and resilience of all children navigating grief.

A childhood bereavement policy will provide a structure for what support might look like and enable a setting-wide approach to be implemented and communicated to others. We have talked through many complexities of death and bereavement such as after a long illness, through suicide and in military combat and suggested elements to include in your document for each of these eventualities as well as signposting to key resources in order for schools to feel supported in writing their own meaningful policy.

Bereaved children, particularly those who are neurodivergent and those with life-limiting conditions may experience heightened awareness of their own mortality. Special schools and hospices play a pivotal role in supporting these children, and we are privileged to be able to share their insights with you in our book. We have also identified the additional considerations of support that may be needed for grieving children from different minority groups, whose experiences are greatly influenced by their culture. The minority groups include those from ethnic minorities, families from Roma Communities or Traveller groups and prison-experienced families.

The experience of grief is unique, often painful and impacts our lives from the point of loss, forevermore. Grief is an uninvited companion with whom we must navigate our life moving forward. The person we love has died and they will not return. Our memories are what we hold onto and some feel a spiritual connection, while others find comfort in the legacy or the impact of a person's written works, artistic endeavours or family traits seen in others. Many find solace in both. What grief can provide is compassion for others in a similar situation, and our experiences can support those who have not yet been on this journey. It is in this vein we have included lived experiences of those who were bereaved as children or who have supported their own children and the children they teach. We hope that an awareness of their experiences will guide you in your own planning to support bereaved children.

Teaching is demanding at the best of times, and supporting bereaved children on top of a challenging role can feel overwhelming. We cannot emphasise enough how crucial self-care is. We offer practical strategies tailored for educators, such as establishing professional boundaries, seeking support from colleagues and mental health professionals, practising mindfulness and engaging in activities that promote well-being. It is also important to recognise personal triggers and seek professional help whenever it is needed.

As a busy and relatively inexperienced teacher I was grateful for the support I received from a governor when first navigating how best to support a bereaved child. She provided a number of useful books and signposted me to helpful organisations. I hope that this is something we have achieved in Chapter 13, it can be daunting to know where to begin, so I hope our small selection of books to use in the classroom is a useful starting point as well as our short directory of bereavement charities. For those interested in reading further our short reading list of freely available online articles should prove helpful and the websites provided have a number of further resources available.

Throughout this book, we emphasise the need for open, honest conversations about death, and fostering a compassionate and understanding school environment where grieving students feel safe and supported. As teachers we are not trying to 'cure' grief but instead in the words of Alan D. Wolfelt, Ph.D. 'bear witness, learn, and accompany' acknowledging that:

'Grievers are the experts of their own experience. Companions offer a safe space, an open heart, affirmation, and hope'. Alan D. Wolfelt, Ph.D. (no date).

**Supporting bereaved pupils does not require a specialist, all school staff are well placed to be a companion, walking alongside those children who may be grieving, with compassion and curiosity.**

## Bibliography

Wolfelt, A.D. (no date). *Tenets of companioning the bereaved*. Available at: https://www.taps.org/globalassets/pdf/covid/tenets-of-companioning (Accessed: 3 February 2025).

# CHILDREN'S ADVICE TO SCHOOL ADULTS

'What can adults in school do to help children whose family member has died?'

Adults in school can help by listening and allowing us to talk about our feelings.

Jack, aged 9

the teacher can help by asking how you feel.

Jacob, aged 8

As a teacher to help a child when they are sad because a relative has died you could help support them by asking how they are feeling and regularly checking on them.

Charlie, aged 9

If a child doesn't want to talk about their feelings, let them draw instead

Willow, aged 8

A School adult could talk to the child's parents to find out about the death and how the child cope better.

Grace, aged 9

# Index

activities 88-91, 93, 96, 99, 102
Adams, John 3
afterlife 40-44
anger 21-22, 33, 63
anniversaries 5, 12, 52, 65, 79

Badger's Parting Gifts 12, 92-93
behavioural changes 35-36
bereavement Support Plans 50
Bonanno, George 21-22
Bowlby, John 22
Buddhism 41-42

Child Bereavement UK 46, 81, 108
Childhood Bereavement Policy 46, 48, 53, 113
Children's Psychological Therapies Team 60-61
Christianity 39-40, 45
chronic grief 13, 22
collaborative culture 57
communication 34-36, 55-58
communities 37, 48, 61
complicated grief 13, 16, 22, 66
culture 18, 57-58, 64

death... of a parent 13, 15-16, 43
death...of a sibling 5, 16, 110
delayed grief 5, 13, 15, 22, 55
despair 22, 47
Dual Process Model 22, 30, 50-53

emotional reactions 32, 36, 55
ethnic minority groups 67
exaggerated grief 13

family 16, 19, 25, 61, 88, 94
five stages of grief (Kübler-Ross) 21-22

grief cycles 29
grieving behaviours 16
guilt 12, 15, 17, 22, 33

Hinduism 41
humanism 43, 45, 67

infants 32, 34
Islam 40, 45
isolation 13, 16-17

Judaism 43, 45

Klass, Dennis 21-22, 30
Kübler-Ross, Elisabeth 8, 14, 21, 30

language 27, 29, 67-68
lived experience 24, 75, 77
loneliness 16-17
long term 5, 46
loss 7, 23, 42
Lytje, Martin 49-50, 53

Marfleet Foundation (The) 77, 90, 109
masked grief 13
military bereavement 48, 53
minority groups 66-67

neurodiverse 36-38
neurodiversity 35

organisations 107-110
overwhelmed 57

Parkes, Colin Murray 21-22, 30
parliamentary petition 3
policy 46-51
pre-teens 33-34, 37
prison 71-73
prison-experienced families 6, 68, 70-71, 113
puddle jumping 12, 14, 22, 51

Roma communities 67-68, 113
Rosen, Michael 101-102, 110

Schut, Henk 22, 50-52
Scotty's Little Soldiers 48, 50, 53, 109
self-care 6, 81, 83-85, 113
SEND 35, 54-55, 88
Showmen 68-70

Sikhism 42-43
social aggression 16
special schools 54, 56, 57
staff 61-62, 81
stages of grief 21, 27
Stroebe, Margaret 22, 50-52
support needs 54

teenagers 33, 35
The Invisible String 12, 95-97
toddlers 32, 34
Tonkin, Lois 10, 14
Traveller groups 6, 67-68, 113

welfare 50, 81
wellbeing 26, 38, 86
When They Died 98-99, 110
whole class 2, 31, 36, 37, 110
Winston's Wish 46, 109

For Product Safety Concerns and Information please contact our EU representative GPSR@taylorandfrancis.com
Taylor & Francis Verlag GmbH, Kaufingerstraße 24, 80331 München, Germany

www.ingramcontent.com/pod-product-compliance
Lightning Source LLC
Chambersburg PA
CBHW082101230426
43670CB00017B/2919